DEMOCRACY

EXPLORING WORLD GOVERNMENTS

ABDO
Publishing Company

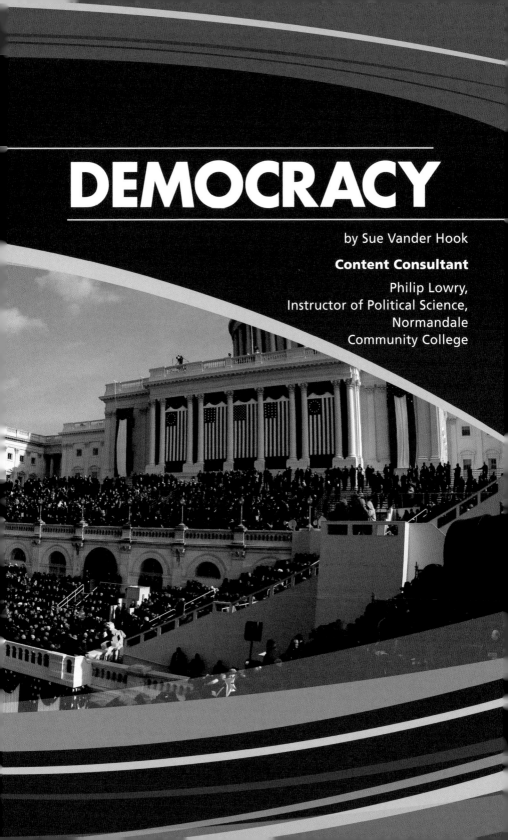

DEMOCRACY

by Sue Vander Hook

Content Consultant

Philip Lowry,
Instructor of Political Science,
Normandale
Community College

CREDITS

Published by ABDO Publishing Company, 8000 West 78th Street, Edina, Minnesota 55439. Copyright © 2011 by Abdo Consulting Group, Inc. International copyrights reserved in all countries. No part of this book may be reproduced in any form without written permission from the publisher. The Essential Library™ is a trademark and logo of ABDO Publishing Company.

Printed in the United States of America,
North Mankato, Minnesota
112010
012011

Editor: Holly Saari
Copy Editor: Amy E. Quale
Interior Design and Production: Becky Daum
Cover Design: Becky Daum

Photo Credits: Elise Amendola/AP Images, cover, 2, 3; Alexander Gardner/Library of Congress, 9; Floriano Rescigno/ iStockphoto, 17; Shutterstock Images, 21, 72, 83; Gianni Dagli Orti/Corbis, 24; iStockphoto, 29; Briggs Co./George Eastman House/Getty Images, 37; Library of Congress, 43, 52, 75, 139; Jean Leon Gerome Ferris/Library of Congress, 46; Rich Koele/ iStockphoto, 55; Julie Jacobson/AP Images, 59; Jarno Gonzalez Zarraonandia/Shutterstock Images, 61; Toru Yamanaka/AFP/ Getty Images, 65; Emin Kuliyev/Shutterstock Images, 79; Bain News Service/Library of Congress, 89; AP Images, 99, 125; Eric Risberg/AP Images, 105; J Pat Carter/AP Images, 110; Virginia Mayo/AP Images, 113; Ken Tannenbaum/Shutterstock Images, 123; Nick Pavlakis/Shutterstock Images, 135

Library of Congress Cataloging-in-Publication Data
Vander Hook, Sue, 1949-
  Democracy / by Sue Vander Hook.
    p. cm. -- (Exploring world governments)
  Includes bibliographical references.
  ISBN 978-1-61714-790-6
  1. Democracy. 2. Democracy--History. I. Title.
  JC423.V347 2011
  321.8--dc22
                                        2010039490

Table of Contents

INTRODUCTION	What Is Government?	6
CHAPTER 1	Power to the People	8
CHAPTER 2	Democracy's Foundation	16
CHAPTER 3	Traces of Democracy	28
CHAPTER 4	Revolutions for Democracy	42
CHAPTER 5	How Democracy Works	54
CHAPTER 6	Types of Democracy	64
CHAPTER 7	Individual Rights	74
CHAPTER 8	The Right to Vote	88
CHAPTER 9	Economic Systems	104
CHAPTER 10	Democracies on the World Stage	112
CHAPTER 11	Dominant Democracy	124
CHAPTER 12	Free to Criticize	134

QUICK FACTS	144
GLOSSARY	148
ADDITIONAL RESOURCES	150
SOURCE NOTES	152
INDEX	157

What Is Government?

In the earliest, simplest societies, government as we know it did not exist. Family or tribal elders made decisions, and their powers were limited. As civilizations grew, governments developed to organize societies and to protect them from outside threats. As societies have grown in complexity, so have the governments that organize them. In this way, organizing society has led to massive bureaucracies with many offices and roles.

As of 2010, there were more than 190 countries, each with its own government. Two governments may look very similar on paper even though political life inside those countries varies greatly. Every government is different because it is influenced by its country's history, culture, economics, geography, and even psychology.

Still, governments share some main roles. Today, a main function of governments is to protect citizens from outside threats. This has evolved into the vast arena of international relations, including military alliances and trade agreements. Governments also organize power in a society. However, how power is acquired—through elections, heredity, or force—varies, as does who exercises it—one person, a few, or many.

Ideally, governments balance the rights of individuals against the needs of the whole society. But who defines those needs? Is it leaders chosen by universal suffrage, or is it a single dictator who assumed power through force? How are individual rights protected? The answers to these questions distinguish one form of government from another.

Another role of government is preserving internal order—that is, order as defined by those in power. While keeping order might mean prosecuting violent criminals in a democracy, in a dictatorship, it could mean prosecuting dissenters. Governments also look out for the welfare of their citizens. All modern governments provide some form of social services, ranging from education to housing to health care.

Governments are often involved in their national economies. Involvement can run the full spectrum—from completely planning the economy to merely levying taxes and allowing a free market to operate. Governments also regulate the private lives of citizens—from issuing marriage licenses in a democracy to enforcing specific styles of dress in a theocracy.

While all governments have some characteristics in common, the world's governments take many forms and make decisions differently. How does a government decide what individual rights to give its citizens? How are laws enforced? What happens when laws are broken? The answers to such questions depend on the political system at hand. ⌘

1

Power to the People

The ancient Greeks, in the first known democratic society, called their form of government *dēmokratía*. It is a combination of the Greek words *demos*, meaning "people," and *krátos*, meaning "rule." In 1863, US President Abraham Lincoln stated the importance of democracy in the country. He delivered his Gettysburg Address in the midst of the American Civil War, at a time when the country was on the verge of splitting. In his speech, he fervently urged some 15,000 listeners to dedicate themselves to democracy, so that "government

At the site of the Battle of Gettysburg, President Lincoln delivered a memorable speech about democracy and the importance of freedom.

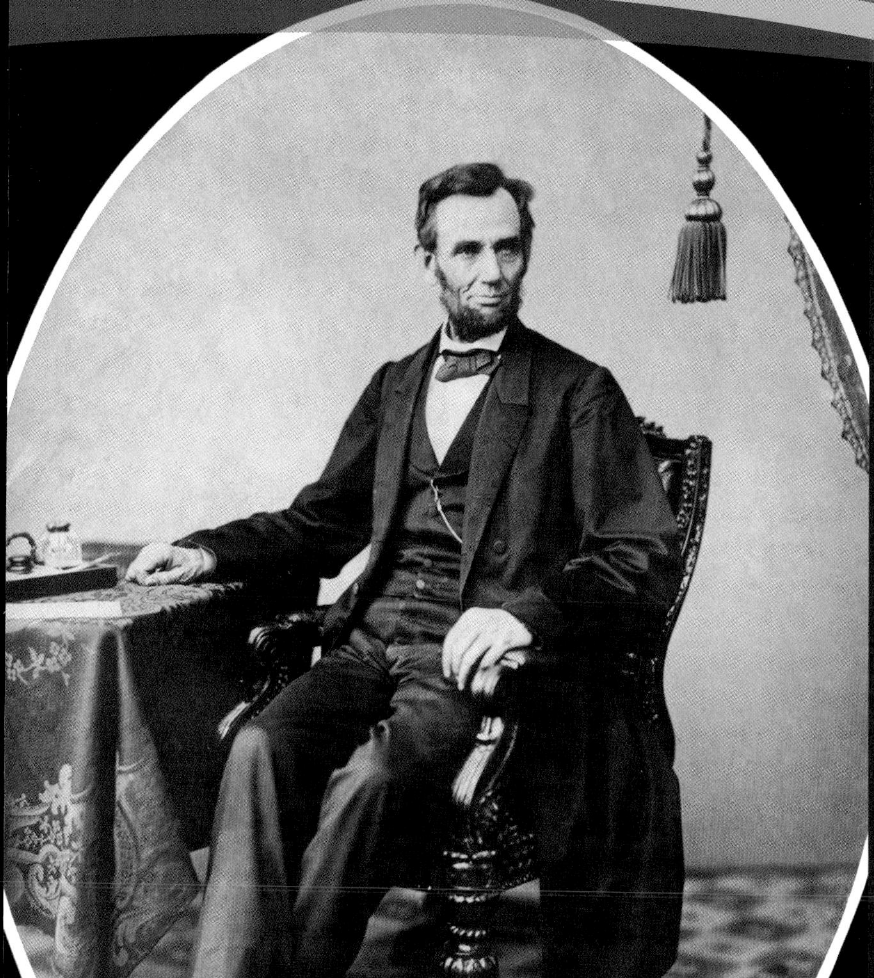

of the people, by the people, for the people shall not perish from the earth."[1]

Democracy Defined

Democracy can be defined as a government in which citizens govern themselves. It is a political system in which absolute power resides with the people, who have the right either to vote individually or to elect people to represent them and vote on their behalf in fair, competitive elections. In a pure, or direct, democracy, the power to govern lies directly in the hands of the people, who vote individually on each issue. James Madison, the fourth president of the United States, wrote in *The Federalist* in 1787 that a pure democracy is "a society consisting of a small number of citizens, who assemble and administer the government in person."[2] Most democracies, however, are a representative form of democracy. In the representative form of democracy, people elect representatives to

THE FEDERALIST

The Federalist (later called *The Federalist Papers*) was a collection of 85 essays written between October 1787 and August 1788. The essays encouraged ratification of the Constitution of the United States of America. Written by many founding fathers of the United States, the collection presents a clear explanation of a democratic system of government.

act and vote on their behalf and in their interests.

It is commonly agreed that a democracy includes two basic principles: freedom and equality. In the fourth century BCE, ancient Greek philosopher Aristotle wrote in his book *Politics*, "For if liberty and equality . . . are chiefly to be found in democracy, they will be best attained when all persons alike share in the government to the utmost."[3] Thousands of years later, the American Declaration of Independence, written by Thomas Jefferson in 1776, included the same basic principles of liberty and equality to describe democracy.

Spread of Democracy

For the past two centuries, democracy has become increasingly popular, with the form of government spreading throughout the world. In 1999, Amartya Sen, winner of the Nobel Prize in Economics, was asked to state the most important event of the twentieth century. He said,

> The past hundred years are not lacking in important events. Nevertheless, among the great variety of developments that have occurred in the twentieth century, I did not, ultimately, have any difficulty in choosing one as the preeminent development of the period: the rise of democracy.[4]

Sen added that during the twentieth century, democracy reached billions of people with a variety of histories, cultures, religions, and social classes. He claimed that when people look back at the twentieth century, they will regard democracy as the most acceptable form of government.

Since 1974, democracy has spread throughout the world more rapidly than at any other time in history. According to Freedom House, an organization that tracks freedom and democracy throughout the world, there were 116 democracies as of 2009—approximately 60 percent of the world's countries.[5]

FREEDOM HOUSE: WATCHDOG OF FREEDOM

Americans concerned about rising threats to democracy and freedom founded Freedom House in 1941. The first co-chairpersons were Eleanor Roosevelt and Wendell Willkie. Freedom House rates countries as free, partly free, or not free. From 1972 through 2009, the number of free countries in the world increased by 46 percent, from 44 to 89 countries. Partly free countries rose 30 percent, from 38 to 58 countries. Not free countries declined 24 percent, from 69 to 47 countries. In 2009, 116 countries had democratic governments.[6]

However, from 2005 to 2009, the number of democratic countries declined, dropping from 119 to 116, the lowest since 1995.[7]

Freedom ratings were lowered for 40 countries in Africa, Latin America, the Middle East, and Eastern Europe. The Middle East was labeled the most repressive region in the world. Freedom House Executive Director Jennifer Windsor stated,

> In 2009, we saw a disturbing erosion of some of the most fundamental freedoms. . . . From the brutal repression on the streets of Iran, to the sweeping detention of Charter 08 [democracy movement] members in China and murders of journalists and human rights activists in Russia, we have seen a worldwide crackdown against individuals asserting their universally accepted rights over the last five years.[8]

The Path of Democracy

Since its inception in the Greek city-state of Athens more than 2,500 years ago, democracy has taken many shapes and forms. After Athens was conquered, democracy disappeared for approximately 1,500 years, reappearing in traces in the thirteenth century and during the Renaissance and fully reemerging in the late eighteenth century when the United States of America formed. Throughout the nineteenth and twentieth centuries, more countries established governments ruled by the people.

Following World War II, toppled dictatorships in Western Europe and Japan gave way to democracies. Communism, however, was also spreading. The Soviet bloc formed after the war and placed Eastern European countries under totalitarian rule. In the mid-1970s, communism also triumphed in South Vietnam and Cambodia in the aftermath of the Vietnam War. But in the 1970s, democracies began to rise at a steady rate. In 1991, the Soviet Union dissolved, and the number of democratic nations surged. All 15 Communist countries that had made up the Soviet Union adopted democratic forms of government. Countries such as Poland, Hungary, and the Czech Republic, starved for individual and political freedoms, welcomed governments run by the people.

In 2006, the number of democracies in the world peaked at 123 nations, but over the following three years, seven of those countries would no longer be democracies.[9] A number of factors can cause a democracy to fail. Democracy is a fragile government, capable of collapsing when political powers get out of balance or when a country's economy is at risk. In June 2010, the European Union's Commission President José Manuel Barroso warned that democracy could disappear in Greece, Spain, and Portugal. He attributed the impending failure to enormous national debts, governments that were running out of money, and economies on the verge of collapse.[10] Although a democratic constitution protects the rights and freedoms of a country's citizens, unexpected crises can weaken a democracy, making it vulnerable to dictators, military coups, or citizen uprisings.

KENNEDY ON DEMOCRACY

"Democracy is the superior form of government, because it is based on a respect for man as a reasonable being."[11]

—*John F. Kennedy, in his senior thesis,* Why England Slept, *1940*

The nineteenth and twentieth centuries came to be called the age of democracy. It was a period of time when democracy brought freedom and equality to millions of people and allowed them to have voices in their governments. The beginning of the twenty-first century saw a slight decline in democracies. It was significant enough, however, to cause the world to take notice. It was enough to encourage nations and independent organizations, such as the National Endowment for Democracy and Freedom House, to keep a close watch on democracy and make every effort to preserve freedom throughout the world. ⌘

FREEDOM FOR ALL?

The language of the American Declaration of Independence left out two groups: women and African Americans. In July 1848, US women's rights activist Elizabeth Cady Stanton helped draft a document called the Declaration of Sentiments. It quoted the Declaration of Independence but included women in the language. The sentence read, "We hold these truths to be self-evident, that all men and women are created equal."[12]

In 1963, civil rights leader Martin Luther King Jr. challenged his audience on the steps of the Lincoln Memorial in Washington DC to remember that all races have the right to be free. In his "I Have a Dream" speech, King quoted the Declaration of Independence, but he admonished his audience that "the Negro still is not free."[13] He said,

I have a dream that one day this nation will rise up and live out the true meaning of its creed: "We hold these truths to be self-evident: that all men are created equal."[14]

2

Democracy's Foundation

The dawn of democracy took place in Greece during the sixth century BCE. Hundreds of independent city-states were scattered throughout Greece's landscape of mountains, islands, and peninsulas along the Mediterranean Sea. Some city-states, such as Sparta, Corinth, and Thebes, were just a few of the central cities from which surrounding towns and territories were governed, usually by kings or tyrants. But it was in Athens where democracy began. Although other democracies may have existed

The Parthenon sits atop the Acropolis in Athens, the Greek city where democracy began.

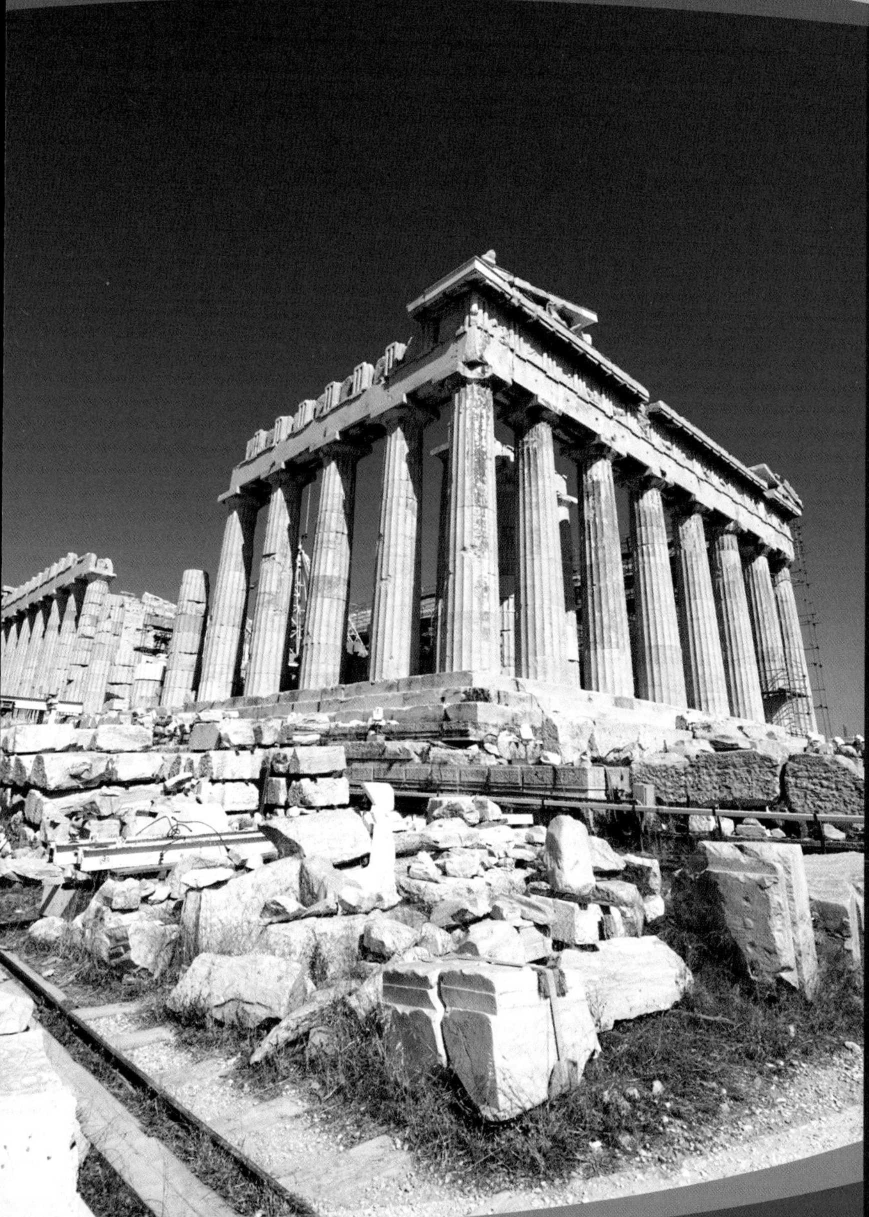

in the ancient world, this city-state is generally considered the government's birthplace.

Overthrowing Tyranny

In 546 BCE, a tyrant named Peisistratos took control of Athens, Greece. When he died, his two sons continued his dictatorial reign of terror until 510 BCE. That year, Cleisthenes, an Athenian aristocrat, led a revolt. Cleisthenes and the people of Athens rioted, climbed the rocky crags of the Acropolis, stormed the temple at the top, and overthrew tyranny. Cleisthenes then wrote a new constitution for Athens that restructured the government, taking power away from one ruler and giving it to the citizens. They called their government democracy—rule by the people. At the end of the fifth century BCE, Greek historian Thucydides wrote about Athens' unique form of government: "Its administration [favors] the many instead of the few; this is why it is called a *democracy*."[1]

More Citizens, But Not Everyone

Before Athens became a democracy, the only legal citizens were men who descended from the four original Athenian tribes, the chief aristocratic families. Cleisthenes's constitution ended this tribal structure and divided Athens into ten districts. Cleisthenes hoped to unify the people of Athens and eliminate the divisions of power caused by the tribes. His goal, as he stated, was "to mix them up in order that more might have a share in the government."[2] The constitution abolished last names to eradicate the connection to the old power-based tribes. Instead, people were identified by their districts, where both aristocrats and commoners lived together.

All free men over the age of 18, aristocrats and commoners alike, became citizens of Athens. Citizens could participate in government and own land and slaves. They enjoyed liberty, equality, freedom of speech, and the right to vote in fair elections. However, only approximately

WOMEN IN ATHENS

Although Athenians worshiped many goddesses and held these female figures in high esteem, an ordinary woman was generally of low social status. Women of ancient Athens were honored for their ability to bear children, but overall they were considered weak and untrustworthy.

Women had no political rights, could not be educated, and were considered possessions of their husbands. If a woman was not married, she was the property of her closest male relative. Ancient artwork indicates that Athenian women wore clothing that completely covered their bodies and veiled their faces.

Women were expected to stay home most of the time. A woman could usually go out only if accompanied by her husband or male relative for special occasions such as festivals or funerals. Poorer women were permitted out of the house more because they often worked alongside their husbands and helped them shop for food and gather water. But according to Xenophon, a Greek historian, a woman was made to be inside and perform domestic tasks:

Thus your duty will be to remain indoors . . . and superintend those who are to work indoors. . . . And when wool is brought to you, you must see that cloaks are made for those that want them. You must see too that the dry corn is in good condition for making food.[3]

20 percent of Athenians were citizens. Women were barred from citizenship and could not vote or have a say in political affairs. Slaves, who made up approximately a third of Athenian society, were also denied citizenship.

PERICLES—DEFENDER OF DEMOCRACY

Pericles was the leader of one of the ten districts of Athens in the mid-fifth century BCE. He was one of the greatest defenders and promoters of ancient democracy. Aristotle wrote that under Pericles's leadership, "the masses grew bold, and drew the whole government more into their own hands."[4] Pericles was devoted to maintaining Athens' successful democracy and spreading it to as many neighboring city-states as possible.

The Council of 500 and the Ecclesia

Athens was a direct democracy, with no national leader or elected representatives. Each of the ten districts of Athens was divided into six local units, and each unit had a leader who served much like a modern-day mayor. Each district selected 50 ordinary citizens, chosen randomly each year, to serve on the Council of 500. Council members met together every day. Each month they chose a different person as leader of the council. These 500 citizens handled the affairs of the entire region and helped govern the people.

Pericles was a key figure in the development of democracy.

They prepared the agenda for the Ecclesia, the main decision-making body of Athens.

The Ecclesia, also called the Assembly, was made up of all the citizens of Athens, approximately 6,000 free men. Nearly every week, the Ecclesia met at the Pnyx, a large outdoor arena carved into the side of a hill just west of the Acropolis. There, the 500 members of the council proposed new laws to the Ecclesia and suggested changes and improvements in government. Members of the Ecclesia could also make individual proposals during the meeting. The purpose of the Ecclesia was to have the people govern Athens.

Citizens nominated and voted for leaders, passed legislation, and made final decisions on war and peace.

Speaking

Any citizen could speak at the gatherings of the Ecclesia. When a proposed issue or law was presented, the presiding officer of the Ecclesia opened debate with the invitation, "*Tis agoreyein bouletai?—*Who wishes to speak?"[5] Lively debates ensued. People on both sides of an issue often shouted their arguments at each other. Still, fair debates were encouraged, as the Athenian Diodotus said, "The good citizen ought to triumph not by frightening his opponents but by beating them fairly in argument."[6]

ORATORS

Citizens with strong voices who were skilled at speaking to large crowds were called orators. They often stood on the stone platform at the top of the hill and presented persuasive speeches. There were generally 50 to 100 orators who were comfortable speaking to the entire Ecclesia.

Voting and Legal System

When debate on an issue ended, members of the Ecclesia voted, sometimes by raising their hands and other times by secret ballot. Archaeologists in Athens have uncovered stone ballot boxes and small metal discs. Most likely, each citizen dropped a disc into a ballot box to vote for or against a candidate or proposed legislation.

In Athens, the legal system was designed so citizens could bring charges against other citizens in court. A trial was scheduled, and a jury was called; citizens were selected at random on a daily or weekly basis to serve as jurors. At the end of the trial, the jurors voted.

A Strong Military

In order to preserve democracy, Athenians had to defend themselves from foreign invaders and tyrants. Shortly after the Athenians established their new government, they formed an army of citizen soldiers called hoplites. Hoplites wore heavy armor and carried huge round shields into battle. They were armed with long spears and fought in phalanx formation—a rectangular block of soldiers marching side by side into battle with weapons held high. The Athenians also built a fleet of more than 200 warships.

From 499 to 479 BCE, the Athenian military and democracy were put to the test against Persia, the world's largest and most powerful empire. In 490 BCE, at the Battle of Marathon, Athens' army defeated the mighty Persians. Ten years later, in 480 BCE, the Athenian navy was tested in the Mediterranean Sea. Although vastly outnumbered by Persian ships, the Athenians outmaneuvered the Persians in a strait off the coast of Athens near the island of Salamis. One after another, Athenian warships, propelled by

*A hoplite is the subject of a
fourth century BCE piece of art.*

man-powered oars, rammed Persian ships as they
came through the narrow channel. The Athenians
were victorious after an all-day battle. The Athenian navy had proven strong and unstoppable
and had successfully defended the democratic
city-state.

The Delian League

A confident Athenian navy then went on to liberate other Greek city-states that had been invaded by Persia. Athens and these city-states formed an alliance—the Delian League—to defend each other against future attacks by Persia or other empires. They also agreed to never attack one another. Athens was the head of this mutual defense pact, which eventually grew to include more than 250 Greek city-states.

Residents of the city-states in the Delian League paid taxes, usually in the form of wheat and barley, to fund the alliance and the military. The league treasury was located in Athens. The money helped maintain a strong military and supported Athenian art and architecture. Most people enjoyed the advantages of being part of the league. However, some people objected to paying taxes that mostly benefited Athens.

LAW OF OSTRACISM

Sometimes citizen leaders of Athens became power hungry and took too much authority. In order to prevent this, Athenians passed the law of ostracism, which allowed them to banish a suspicious leader from the city-state. The first man they banished was Hipparchus, a relative of Peisistratos, one of the last tyrants before Athens first became a democracy. For the first three years of their new government, Athenians banished relatives and friends of past tyrants and removed anyone who appeared too powerful.

End of the First Democracy

The end of Athenian democracy began with mistrust and conflict between the Delian League and another alliance of neighboring city-states, called the Peloponnesian League. Sparta, the chief city-state of the Peloponnesian League, resented Athens' power and prosperity. In addition, there were members of the Delian League who were disgruntled with Athens and wanted their independence back. One by one, city-states in both leagues opposed Athens. However, they were all unsuccessful in their attempts to defeat the strong Athenian military.

Conflicts between Athens and Sparta increased, and in 431 BCE, war broke out between the Delian League and the Peloponnesian League. The Peloponnesian War, as it was called, lasted 27 years. In 404 BCE, Athens and its allies surrendered to Sparta, marking the end of the war. Sparta immediately established a government of tyranny, later called the government of the Thirty Tyrants. Freedoms and voting rights were greatly

REMEMBERED BY THE US GOVERNMENT

Over the gallery doors of the US House of Representatives chamber is a marble bas-relief of Lycurgus, a great orator of Athens. It is one of 23 bas-reliefs of historical people noted for their work in establishing the principles upon which US law is based.

reduced for Athenians, and many of them were exiled, thrown in jail, or executed. A year later, the tyrants were overthrown and democracy was reestablished in Athens. In 338 BCE, however, King Philip II of Macedonia conquered all of Greece and brought democracy to an end. ⌘

3

Traces of Democracy

After the Macedonians conquered Athens in 338 BCE, democracy nearly disappeared. Over the next two millennia, only glimmers of democracy were found throughout the world. The governments of some European cities, such as Venice and Florence in Italy, had traces of democracy. For a while, nobles and commoners were represented in politics, but civil wars and conflicts with other empires repeatedly set the stage for strong dictators to rise and rule the world.

Dictatorial rulers, such as Julius Caesar, threatened the survival of democracy.

World of Dictators

Alexander the Great rose to power in Greece in 336 BCE. He began conquering large territories such as Asia Minor, Egypt, Palestine, Babylon, and India. Rome was also vying for world power. For hundreds of years, Rome's representative form of government slowly eroded and gave way to brutal dictators such as Nero, Trajan, Marcus Aurelius, and Julius Caesar. The Roman Republic became the Roman Empire, and totalitarian rulers extended the empire's reign across the

NERO, CRUEL EMPEROR

Nero was the emperor of the Roman Empire from 54 to 68 CE. Although Nero's reign was characterized by fine architecture, art, and athletic games, he is best remembered for his cruel acts. Under his rule, religious persecution was common. Historian Tacitus wrote of Nero's torture and executions of first-century Christians. He states in *The Annals,*

> *Nero fastened the guilt and inflicted the most exquisite tortures on a class hated for their abominations, called Christians. . . . Mockery of every sort was added to their deaths. Covered with the skins of beasts, they were torn by dogs and perished,*

or were nailed to crosses, or were doomed to the flames and burnt, to serve as a nightly illumination, when daylight had expired.[1]

Tacitus also wrote that it was in Rome "where all things hideous and shameful from every part of the world find their centre and become popular."[2] Nero's dictatorship was filled with corruption, affairs, and executions. It was a government controlled by one person unrestricted by law—a political system quite opposite of democracy.

In 68, a military coup overthrew Nero and planned to kill him. Instead, Nero committed suicide by thrusting a dagger into his neck.

known world until 476 CE. At its peak, the Roman Empire controlled most of present-day Europe, the Middle East, and northern Africa; yet, the Empire was marked by wars, slavery, revolts, and corruption.

Other parts of the world had similar autocratic governments. A variety of monarchies, dynasties, and empires spread throughout China, Persia, India, Mexico, Egypt, England, and other countries. In what came to be called the Middle Ages, monarchs and dictators ruled most of the world. When they died, power was often passed down to one of their children, keeping despotism alive for centuries.

Local Equality

During the Middle Ages, when dictators ruled most of the world, Scandinavian communities in the far north had governments ruled by the people. Equality was important to citizens of Denmark, Norway, Sweden, Switzerland, and the Netherlands. Small communities created local democratic gatherings—called *things*—in which free men could discuss issues and existing laws. At the end of the thirteenth century, communities in rural areas of Switzerland

SCANDINAVIAN DEMOCRACY

The old tradition of the thing, the local democratic meeting in Scandinavian countries, is still reflected today. The parliament of Iceland is called the *Althing*; in Norway, it is the *Storting* and in Denmark the *Folketing*.

established governments much like the democracy of Athens. Every adult male regularly walked to an open-air assembly to cast his vote.

In northern Italy, there were also traces of democracy. From the eleventh through the thirteenth centuries, communes were a popular phenomenon in the area. Groups of people formed independent communities that grew in wealth and independence. At first, they were established to protect their prosperous trade route, but later they became recognized as legitimate governments. All male citizens participated in these democratic assemblies called *arengos*. Eventually, these democracies evolved into oligarchies, governments ruled by a few powerful people. The few were usually the nobility and wealthy merchants. The only commune that avoided an oligarchy was Venice, which maintained local democratic rule until the eighteenth century. Other democratic communes also emerged in parts of Germany and Spain.

The Magna Carta

As time passed, some monarchs began sharing their power with representatives of the people. Some did it willingly; others were forced to give up some powers by the people themselves. King John of England was one king who was compelled to give up some of his power. His reign and his forced relinquishment of powers marked one of the most significant events in the development of democracy.

On June 15, 1215, English nobles took King John to a large tent in a rural meadow called Runnymede. There, they forced him to put his seal on the Magna Carta, a handwritten document that proclaimed certain rights for all free men of England. Toward the beginning, the document states, "To all free men of our kingdom we have also granted, for us and our heirs for ever, all the liberties written out below."[3] The Magna Carta bound King John and all heirs to his throne to maintain the freedoms and limitations set forth in the document.

The Magna Carta protected and gave rights to free people, but very few people, in fact, were free. Most of the people of England were peasants or slaves, and neither group was considered free. Free men included nobles, landowners, some religious leaders, and a few commoners with prominent government positions—and only men. The Magna Carta essentially was a long list of grievances English nobles had against their king. It limited the power of the king, set up fair legal procedures, and barred the monarch from interfering with the Catholic Church. At the time, some leaders of the church held powerful positions in government.

Many people consider the Magna Carta the most important legal document in the history of democracy. It was the spark that would one day set afire people's movements to be free and have voices in their governments. The Magna Carta states,

No freeman shall be taken, imprisoned . . . or in any other way destroyed . . . except by the lawful judgment of his peers, or by the law of the land. To no one will we sell, to none will we deny or delay, right or justice.[4]

Later, democratic constitutions would emulate the language of the Magna Carta and contain similar declarations of rights and freedoms.

English noblemen continued to work toward democratic principles for their country. England's first Parliament, or legislative body, met in 1246. At first, Parliament was a group that merely advised the king, but gradually, the king's authority diminished and the authority of Parliament grew. In 1258, members of Parliament forced King Henry III to allow them to meet every three years to discuss and decide national issues.

In Spain and Portugal, parliaments were established in which representatives of the people voted on legislation, sometimes with more power than the king or the queen. In France, King Louis IX allowed a parliament, called the Parlement of

CHURCHILL ON THE MAGNA CARTA

In 1956, more than 700 years after the Magna Carta was signed, British Prime Minister Winston Churchill praised the document:

Here is a law which is above the King and which even he must not break. This reaffirmation of a supreme law and its expression in a general charter is the great work of Magna Carta.[5]

Paris, to be established on a permanent basis. Parlement members were to meet four times a year in his palace in Paris. In the late fifteenth century, Poland established an important assembly called the *sejm*. Members of the assembly represented the entire citizenry of Poland. No new law could be passed without the authority of the sejm. But despite democratic progress, monarchs still ruled, and kingdoms and empires continued to battle for world dominance.

The Renaissance

In Europe, a new cultural movement—the Renaissance—arose after the Middle Ages. From the fourteenth to the seventeenth centuries, the movement revitalized learning and art and renewed interest in ancient Greek writings and ideals. People searched through libraries for obscure, ancient texts and began thinking more openly about politics, science, religion, and art.

Many people read the writings of Athenian historian Thucydides and Greek philosophers, such as Plato and Aristotle. These ancient Greeks often wrote about democracy and attempted to explain it. Thucydides described it thoroughly in his *History of the Peloponnesian War*. Aristotle wrote about Athenian government in his *Constitution of Athens*. Even though Plato was a critic of democracy, his well-known *Republic* described the democratic process and provided a glimpse into Athenian democracy.

While the Renaissance has been called a revolution of the intellect, it was also the

DEMOCRATIZATION OF KNOWLEDGE

The development of the printing press by Johannes Gutenberg in 1439 allowed the rapid spread of new ideas during the Renaissance. Common people, not just priests and scholars, could buy books and learn about ideas, such as democracy. In fact, the right to knowledge for all people was in itself a characteristic of democracy. The printing press was one of the first steps toward what came to be called the democratization of knowledge.

beginning of a political awakening. Glimmers of democracy began to spread throughout Europe. Although power still remained in the hands of a few, democratic reforms and freedoms crept into governments and societies. For instance, in Florence, Italy, in the late fifteenth and early sixteenth centuries, top government rulers and the Catholic Church worked together to develop a political system that promoted liberty and some citizen participation.

The American Colonies

While nations of the world juggled monarchies and tried to satisfy people's desire for freedom, King James I of England made a decision that would change the course of democracy's history. On April 10, 1606, he approved the First Charter of Virginia. It granted a group of merchants, called the Virginia Company, the right to "begin their Plantation and Habitation in some fit and convenient Place . . . alongst the Coasts of Virginia, and the coasts of America."[6] The king of

Colonists landed in what became Jamestown Colony in 1607.

England gave the colony the legal right to exist and guaranteed the colonists the privileges of English citizens.

Jamestown Colony, as it was called, was established in 1607 on the East Coast of America. The colonists were allowed to govern themselves without interference from the British monarchy. Jamestown Colony was allowed a representative form of government in which the people would vote for a select few to govern. The charter reads,

> *Each of the said Colonies shall have a Council, which shall govern and order all Matters-and Causes. . . . Each of which Councils shall consist of thirteen Persons, to be ordained, made, and removed, from time to time.*[7]

The Jamestown council, a locally elected governing body, met for the first time in 1619. It would eventually be called the House of Burgesses. The representative body was a model for the foundation of democracy of the United States.

Jamestown Colony also had other elements of democracy. It was allowed a system of free enterprise. Colonists could mine for gold, silver, or copper and use the profits to benefit themselves. Colonists also grew and exported tobacco internationally, making a profit and improving their way of life. They created their own laws and set up their own security and defense systems to protect them from attacks or invasions.

More Traces of Democracy

Other groups of colonists also came to North America in the seventeenth century. In 1620, a group of colonists, later known as the Pilgrims, came to America aboard the *Mayflower*. They were escaping religious persecution and looking for a place to worship as they pleased.

Before the Pilgrims landed and established Plymouth Colony in Massachusetts, 41 passengers signed the Mayflower Compact. It acknowledged their allegiance to King James I but declared their right to "enact, constitute, and frame such just and equal laws, ordinances, acts, constitutions and offices."[8] They established a democratic form of government based on majority rule. Their political system would be a model for future democracies.

In 1682, William Penn founded the colony of Pennsylvania. King Charles II of England had granted Penn a royal charter, which granted the colony the right to exist, but Penn also created a constitution for the colony. It was called the Frame of Government of Pennsylvania. It included freedom of worship, trial by jury, freedom of the press, and the right to propose legislation. It provided for a governor, a governing council to propose legislation, and a General Assembly of 500 to approve it. With each American colony, democracy grew and permeated the lives of thousands of colonists.

Democratic Ideas from England

America was not the only place where democracy was taking hold. In England, during the seventeenth century, authors and historians wrote about democratic ideals. Common people began exploring the writings of people such as English philosopher Thomas Hobbes. In 1651, Hobbes wrote *Leviathan*; in this work,

BLOWS AGAINST DEMOCRACY

The representative side of England's government took several blows in the seventeenth century. In 1622, King James I dissolved Parliament, England's legislative body. In 1641, the Star Chamber, England's court of law, was abolished following accusations that it was corrupt under the rule of King Charles I. The following year, the British revolted against King Charles; civil war broke out and lasted nine years. In the end, the people were victorious; King Charles was beheaded and the monarchy abolished. The British people enjoyed a democratic form of government for a few years, but in 1661, another king—King Charles II—was crowned king of England.

he defended monarchs, but depicted them as Leviathans, or huge monsters. He supported a strong central authority but also championed the rights of the individual and promoted equality and freedom for all men. He believed in representative government in which representatives voted based on the will of the people.

Nearly 40 years later, England made great strides toward democracy. In 1689, Parliament passed the Bill of Rights, a list of rights that entitled English citizens to certain freedoms. They included the right to petition the king and the right to bear arms for defense. A similar document called the Claim of Right was also passed that year in Scotland. The documents would lay the foundation for the US Bill of Rights established a century later.

Members of Parliament now had a stronger voice in government, and opposing viewpoints naturally emerged. It became a tradition for members with one opinion to sit to the right of the Speaker of Parliament; those with an opposite viewpoint sat to the left. It would eventually evolve into what is known as a two-party or multiparty political system.

More Colonial Charters

During the reign of King Charles II, more charters were granted to establish colonies in America. In 1662, King Charles granted the Connecticut Colony a charter that included the right of self-government—autonomous of overseas England—and the privilege of electing a governor.

The Rhode Island charter in 1663 also allowed self-government and the right to elect a governor. Charters allowed colonies to be established all along the Atlantic Coast of North America and to have a certain amount of self-government.

In the late seventeenth century, King James II rescinded most of the colonial charters in order to take more control of the colonies. Leaders of the Connecticut Colony refused to give up their charter. The colonists had tasted freedom and self-government, and they were not willing to give them up.

Colonial Alliance

By the 1760s, more than 2 million colonists lived in America. The colonies were independent of each other until Pennsylvania statesman Benjamin Franklin led efforts to form a colonial union. The colonies' alliance with one another grew stronger as the British restricted them more. Great Britain took away the colonists' self-government, stripped them of their rights and freedoms, and imposed unreasonable taxes on them. The colonists protested, but the British government ignored their complaints. The colonists refused to give up their independence and formed illegal bodies of elected representatives known as Provincial Congresses. Britain tried to gain more control, and the colonists revolted. It brought the second wave of democracy in the world, but it would come only after a bloody revolution that would free the colonists from British rule. ⌘

4

Revolutions for Democracy

Throughout the 1760s, Britain's despotic rule over the American colonists escalated, hindering the colonists' individual freedoms by imposing more laws from overseas. A clash with British soldiers on March 5, 1770, at what came to be called the Boston Massacre, sparked all-out rebellion against Britain. British soldiers killed five colonists, and the colonists' anger at the British monarchy grew. On December 16, 1773, a group of colonists boarded a British ship and dumped its cargo of tea into the harbor. It

In an act of rebellion against the British monarchy, American colonists participated in the Boston Tea Party.

became known as the Boston Tea Party and was another event leading toward revolution.

More oppressive British laws followed: the Sugar Act, the Currency Act, the Stamp Act, and the Townshend Act levied taxes on everything from food and paper to glass and tea. The colonists were angry; taxes were taking most of their money, and they had no voice in British Parliament. The colonists sent petitions and pleas to the king to lighten their tax burden, but the king ignored their requests. The colonists protested passionately. Leaders such as Patrick Henry and James Otis rallied the people to revolt.

The Colonies Unite

Meanwhile, colonists worked to strengthen the democratic assemblies they had already created—local governments called Provincial Congresses. On September 5, 1774, 55 local representatives from all the colonies but Georgia met to discuss collective action against Great Britain. It was called the First Continental Congress. Patrick Henry proclaimed unity and said, "The distinctions between Virginians, Pennsylvanians, New Yorkers, and New Englanders are no more. I am not a Virginian but an American."[1]

Now united, the colonists protested taxation in a document called the Declaration of Rights and Grievances. They also banned imports and exports between England and the colonies and learned the power of a boycott. The colonists' refusal to buy British products hurt England's economy. It also strengthened the colonists' determination to be independent and to govern themselves.

In 1775, the colonists met again at the Second Continental Congress. There, they approved a Continental army and appointed George Washington as its commanding general. In the spring of 1776, Washington and his army forced British soldiers out of Boston, Massachusetts, where they had taken up residence in people's homes.

Declaration of Independence

On July 4, 1776, the 13 American colonies formally became a government of and for the people. They declared their independence from England in a written document called the Unanimous Declaration of the Thirteen United States of America, later called the Declaration of Independence. Its primary author, Thomas Jefferson, hated and feared the British Empire. He dreamed of an America dedicated to liberty, and he believed the colonists had the natural right to govern themselves. The Declaration of Independence

THE COMMITTEE OF FIVE

The Committee of Five was a group of colonists who wrote and presented the Declaration of Independence to the Second Continental Congress on July 4, 1776. The five included John Adams, Roger Sherman, Robert Livingston, Benjamin Franklin, and Thomas Jefferson. The committee gave Jefferson the job of writing the first draft. Only minor changes were made before the final document was finalized and signed.

Benjamin Franklin, John Adams, and Thomas Jefferson wrote and reviewed drafts of the Declaration of Independence.

explains that it was necessary for citizens "to dissolve the political bands which have connected them with another."[2] The second paragraph describes the true essence of the democracy they hoped for:

We hold these truths to be self-evident, that all men are created equal, that they are endowed by their Creator with certain unalienable Rights, that among these are Life, Liberty and the pursuit of Happiness. —That to secure these rights, Governments are instituted among Men, deriving their just powers from the consent of the governed.[3]

The Declaration of Independence makes it clear that it was the colonists' right to overthrow despotic rule to gain back their freedoms: "Whenever any Form of Government becomes destructive of these ends, it is the Right of the People to alter or to abolish it, and to institute new Government."[4] The document continues, "It is their right, it is their duty to throw off such Government."[5]

For the next five years, an untrained American ragtag army fought the mighty British military on land and at sea. Most of the colonists, called patriots, wanted independence and fought for it fiercely and against all odds. On October 19, 1781, British General Charles Cornwallis surrendered his army to the Americans at Yorktown, Virginia. It marked the end of the American Revolution and a victory for America. On September 3, 1783, members of American and British delegations signed the Treaty of Paris, formally ending the war. The last British soldiers left American soil on November 25, 1783.

America was now free. Nearly four years later, the people created their supreme law of the land, the Constitution of the United States of America. Democracy would be the government's firm foundation, and the Constitution was crafted to protect the people against monarchies, dictatorships, and government corruption. The government established was not a direct democracy such as the one in Athens, but a democracy in which the people would elect government representatives who would vote on their behalf. Author Thomas Paine, in his 1792 book *Rights of Man*, called it "representation ingrafted upon democracy," or representation joined together with a democracy.[6]

NATIVE AMERICAN DEMOCRACY

When American colonists developed the government for the newly formed United States of America, the democratic model of the Iroquois Confederacy inspired them. The confederacy was a league of five, and later six, Native American tribes in upper New York State. It included the Mohawks, the Onondagas, the Senecas, the Oneidas, the Cayugas, and the Tuscaroras. Their constitution, the Great Law of Peace, was a model of democracy.

Leaders of each community formed the Grand Council, which consisted of 50 sachems, or chiefs, from the six nations. The women of the tribal clans selected men to serve as Grand Council chiefs. Regularly, they assembled to reason together and vote on issues. Their goal was to end up with a unanimous vote. Votes were taken until all agreed.

In 1775, American colonists invited leaders of the Iroquois Confederacy to the Second Continental Congress in Philadelphia. Twenty-one Iroquois came and shared ideas about their government—tribes united in a confederacy under a common law and governed by the people. They discussed with the colonists American independence and a new democratic government.

Revolution in France

In 1789, just six years after the official end of the American Revolution and the beginning of US democracy, the people of France revolted. They rebelled against their own government, an absolute monarchy ruled by King Louis XVI since 1774. For centuries, powerful monarchs had reigned supreme in France. Now, economic problems had caused the French king to levy new taxes, which angered the people.

But King Louis's fiscal policies failed to bring France out of an economic slump. In 1789, members of the nobility, officials of the Catholic Church, and the common people clashed over the state of the monarchy. They disagreed on what powers belonged to the people. Some of them formed a new assembly, called the National Assembly, and stormed the Bastille prison on July 14. There were only seven prisoners to release, but the act was a symbol of the masses taking control. Common people, many of them peasants, insisted on a voice in government. The French Revolution had begun.

Declaration of Rights

In August 1789, the French National Assembly, which was made up of representatives of the people, approved the Declaration of the Rights of Man and of the Citizen, which was democratic in nature. It established the basic rights for citizens of France, although it excluded any rights for women or slaves. The declaration shares some principles with the American Declaration of Independence. It proclaimed certain natural rights to life, liberty, and property. It states that the role of government, which should be carried out by elected representatives, is to protect these rights. The document proclaims,

> Men are born and remain free and equal in rights. . . . The aim of all political association is the preservation of the natural and impre- scriptible [above the law] rights of man. These rights are liberty, property, security, and resis- tance to oppression.[7]

The document includes freedom of speech, freedom of religion, and freedom of the press. It gives every citizen the right to participate in lawmaking, either directly or through a repre- sentative. Power is given to the people: "The principle of all sovereignty resides essentially in the nation. No body nor individual may exercise any authority which does not proceed directly from the nation."[8]

Uncontrollable Masses

The French people's demand for a democratic style of government grew in intensity as the years passed. They despised the monarchy and treated King Louis and his wife, Marie Antoinette, badly. The masses became more radical and uncontrol- lable. As the National Assembly was crafting a people's constitution in 1791, the king and the queen attempted to flee Paris. However, they were arrested, brought back, and placed under house arrest.

In August 1792, King Louis was arrested and taken to a Paris prison. On September 21, the National Assembly abolished the monarchy and declared France a republic with a representative form of government. In December, the king was brought to trial on charges of high treason and crimes against the state. He was found guilty and given the death penalty. On January 21, 1793, while crowds cheered, King Louis XVI was beheaded by a guillotine.

The conflict was not over, however. Neighboring European countries were outraged that the French people had executed their king. They took up arms against the revolutionaries of France. Factions within France also fought against each other. France was now ruled by a group of men called the Directory, who tried to govern and fight a war at the same time. For nearly a year, they systematically

THE HAITIAN REVOLUTION

During the French Revolution, the people of another nation—the French-owned island of Haiti—rose up against their government. With fiery passion, more than 100,000 slaves rebelled against the French. They burned every plantation on the island and executed every French person they encountered. On January 1, 1804, Haiti declared itself a free republic. It was the first free nation in Latin America and the only independent black-led country in the world. Haiti became a model for other slave rebellions around the globe.

The French Revolution was violent and bloody, but it ushered in some democratic principles.

executed all potential enemies. It was later called the Reign of Terror. In the last six weeks of their reign, about 1,400 people were beheaded by guillotine in Paris alone. The guillotine became a symbol of the French Revolution.

Positive Outcomes

Although the French Revolution appeared to be a failure, it had sweeping, long-lasting effects. The bourgeoisie, or middle class, and the landowners became the dominant political powers. The people of France were united, and feudalism—a political system in which lords owned property and gave land to vassals in exchange for military support—disappeared. Liberty, equality, and unity became important. In 1794, slavery in France was abolished, and blacks were given equal rights. The women of France, however, would not have the right to vote until 1944.

Most important, the French Revolution ushered in democratic elements. The country now had fair elections, a constitution created by the people, and a representative form of government. Inspired by the French and the American Revolutions, other democracies would unfold around the world; the two revolutions laid the foundation for democracy to spread. Over the next century, revolutions sprang up against monarchs who systematically lost more and more power. By the end of the nineteenth century, nearly all Western European countries had constitutions that limited the powers of the monarch and increased the rights of the people. Parliaments and legislatures were established, and democracies emerged. ⌘

5

How Democracy Works

As democracy spread throughout the world in the nineteenth and twentieth centuries, it took on a variety of forms. The United States adopted a representative form of democracy in which the people elect government officials— senators, representatives, and the president. Other nations, such as Canada and India, adopted a parliamentary democracy with an elected parliament that, in turn, elected the country's executive leaders. Some nations, such as Great Britain, Japan, Spain, Australia, and Scandinavian countries, chose constitutional monarchies. They

The US Constitution outlines the democratic principles upon which the United States was founded.

We the People

insure domestic Tranquility, provide for the common defense

and our Posterity, do ordain and establish this Constitution

Article. I.

retained a monarch but limited his or her powers and expanded the power of the people and their elected representatives. A direct democracy, the Athenian model where citizens individually made decisions for their country, was established in the smaller country of Switzerland. Despite their differences, though, democracies around the world shared many common elements.

Constitution—The Supreme Law of the Land

Democracies usually have a constitution that sets up a government structure and protects the freedoms and equality of citizens. The constitution forms the supreme law of the land. In other words, the constitution sets up the power structures of the government and the foundation for its federal laws. The people of ancient Athens fashioned a constitution that allowed every citizen to vote on every issue and every law.

When the United States drafted a constitution in 1787, representatives from the states met to discuss which type of government was best for the new country.

"THE MOST WONDERFUL WORK"

Ninety years after the drafting of the US Constitution, England's Prime Minister William Gladstone reflected on the document and called it "the most wonderful work ever struck off at a given time by the brain and purpose of man."[1]

The constitution they created focused on checks and balances. Equal branches of government questioned and challenged each other to prevent corruption. Citizens were given the right to vote, although women and slaves were excluded.

European Constitutions

In 1791, Poland adopted what would become Europe's oldest democratic constitution. Poland's constitution provided political equality between nobility and townspeople. Peasants were placed under the protection of the government, which reduced the terrible abuses of the forced labor practices of serfdom. Poland retained its king, but democratic reforms greatly diminished corruption in the government.

Other nations were inspired to create their own democratic constitutions. Some countries, such as Norway and Switzerland, already had governments with democratic principles. These countries noticed the success of the US Constitution and wanted to create their own written constitutions to strengthen their democratic ideals.

Representatives of Norway met to draft a constitution in 1814, which was modeled after the US Constitution. Norway's constitution included a balanced separation of powers between executive, legislative, and judicial branches of government. Norway's form of democracy allowed for a monarch, but the king's powers were extremely limited. The constitution also ensured individual freedoms, such as freedom of speech.

In 1848, Switzerland, also inspired by the United States, adopted a new constitution. The document gave individuals the right to participate in public affairs and divided the federal government into executive, legislative, and judicial branches.

Equally Qualified to Vote

Although every democratic constitution is different, they all have at least one basic principle that identifies them as a democracy: All voters have an equally important voice in the political system. Every citizen is deemed equally qualified to participate in the country's decision-making process.

In representative democracies, such as the United States, citizens elect representatives to vote on their behalf. The people make their views known to their representatives, who then are expected to vote according to the will of the majority of their assigned constituents. In the United States, citizens can bring up new matters to their representatives, who in turn may propose new legislation to Congress.

"The right of citizens of the United States to vote shall not be denied or abridged by the United States or by any State on account of sex. Congress shall have power to enforce this article by appropriate legislation."[2]

—*The Nineteenth Amendment to the US Constitution, 1920*

By participating in elections, voters have a say in how their country's government runs.

This idea dates back to 431 BCE in Athens when Pericles proclaimed in a famous speech:

> *Our ordinary citizens, though occupied with the pursuits of industry, are still fair judges of public matters; . . . instead of looking on discussion as a stumbling-block in the way of action, we think it an indispensable preliminary to any wise action at all.*[3]

Fundamentally Equal

In a democracy, all people are considered fundamentally equal. English philosopher John Locke believed that all people were naturally and inherently equal. In 1835, French political philosopher Alexis de Tocqueville discussed equality in his book *Democracy in America*. He wrote, "[Equality] is universal, it is durable, it constantly eludes all human interference, and all events as well as all men contribute to its progress."[4] He believed that nothing could change the basic tenet that all humans are equal.

Separation of Powers

The US Constitution provided for a central government—the federal government—divided into three branches: legislative, executive, and judicial. Each branch has separate and independent powers and responsibilities; by separating them and balancing their powers, the founding fathers hoped that no branch would dominate, a hope that has largely proven true throughout US history. Other countries with multiple branches include Australia, Costa Rica, France, Germany, and Great Britain, but the US system provides a good example of how power is balanced in a democracy.

In the United States, the president and his or her administration make up the executive branch. The president sets the nation's domestic and international agenda; he or she is also the commander in chief of the military. The legislative branch, called Congress, is divided into two houses: the Senate and the House of Representatives. Its major role is to create and pass legislation. The judicial branch consists of a system of courts that interprets and applies the

The US Congress, which meets at the Capitol in Washington DC, has checks on the judicial and executive branches' powers.

laws to resolve conflicts or disputes. Each branch limits the others in specific ways:

- **Executive checks and balances.** The president's main power over the legislative branch is that he or she can refuse to sign a bill, which is called a veto. In that case, the bill does not become law. The president also can recommend items of legislation, which are then deliberated by Congress. The executive's major influence over the judicial branch is that the president appoints federal judges, including Supreme Court justices.

- **Legislative checks and balances.** The president has the power to veto a bill passed by Congress. However, the bill may not necessarily be dead. The bill can be sent back to Congress. To pass it again, both houses of Congress have to approve it, this time by a two-thirds vote. By overriding a veto, Congress checks the president's power. The legislative branch also controls funding for any executive actions, and, in extreme cases, it may force the president from office through the long and rather complex process of impeachment. The Senate approves treaties the executive branch forms with other nations, and members of the Senate must approve presidential

HOW A BILL BECOMES A LAW

All US legislation has to be passed in identical form and language by both houses of Congress. A bill originates from a variety of sources. An individual citizen or group of citizens can bring a proposed bill to Congress. Members of state legislatures often submit bills. Senators and representatives can originate bills, and even the president or members of the administration can suggest new legislation. A bill is usually given to a committee or subcommittee, who reviews it, perhaps changes it, listens to testimony on why the bill is necessary, and asks questions. Members of the committee or subcommittee then vote to determine if the bill should proceed. If the majority does not vote for the bill to continue, the bill dies. If it passes the committee, the bill is sent to the House of Representatives and put to a vote. If the bill passes the House, it goes on to the Senate. If approved by the Senate, the bill then goes to the president of the United States for signature. A bill becomes law if both houses pass the bill by majority vote and the president signs it.

appointments. Congress holds sway over the judicial branch through the power of impeaching judges as well.

- **Judicial checks and balances.** The president and Senate have the power to appoint federal judges, but the judges then remain in office for life. The judiciary's main power over the other two branches comes in the form of judicial review. The court system can overturn executive or legislative actions—laws— by ruling them unconstitutional.

Separation of powers is an essential component of keeping powers balanced in a democracy. It is a key ingredient to preventing tyranny in government. ⌘

POWER OF IMPEACHMENT

In the United States, removing an elected government official from office requires two steps: impeachment, or a formal accusation, by majority vote of the House of Representatives, and a trial and conviction by a two-thirds vote of the Senate. No US president has ever been removed from office by impeachment proceedings. Presidents Andrew Johnson and Bill Clinton were impeached by the House but acquitted by the Senate. In 1973, impeachment hearings began for President Richard Nixon for obstructing justice and refusing to obey subpoenas in regard to the Watergate investigation. Facing probable impeachment, President Richard Nixon resigned from office in August 1974.

6

Types of Democracy

Proponents of democracy point out that one of its strengths is that it can be fine-tuned for the unique political and social needs of each nation. The people of a country decide what common goals they share, what freedoms are important, and how they will make decisions for their society and government. Because each country is distinctive, there are many varieties of democratic governments throughout the world, although the basic tenets of democracy stay the same.

Japanese Emperor Akihito acts as a symbolic ruler in Japan's constitutional monarchy.

Political philosophers today are still trying to define democracy and put rules and limits on governments run by the people. There are checklists that test a nation to determine if it is, in fact, a democracy. But defining democracy may be one of its greatest enemies. A detailed definition could limit democracy and curtail people's rights and choices in creating their own government.

DEMOCRACY OF SWITZERLAND

Since 1848, Switzerland has had a direct democracy. Today the Swiss people still vote directly on each piece of legislation and have the power to change the constitution. In addition, if a group of citizens can gather 50,000 signatures against a law within 100 days, a national vote is taken, and voters decide by simple majority if the law should stand.

Basic Types of Democracy

Democracies have been placed into three basic categories: direct, indirect, and semi-direct. In a direct democracy, all citizens participate directly in the decision-making process. They make proposals, vote on each piece of legislation, and have the power to change the constitution. Ancient Athens practiced a direct democracy, as did most of the original 13 colonies that became the United States. Colonists met regularly at what were called New England town meetings to vote on local issues and laws and to approve budgets.

In an indirect democracy, often called a representative democracy or a republic, representatives vote on behalf of the people. When the United States became an independent nation, a representative government was established. Town meetings changed from places to vote into discussion forums. In the twenty-first century, town hall meetings have become increasingly popular. Audiences ranging from several hundred to several thousand people have met to voice their opinions to their local, state, or federal representatives. Voting is rare at these meetings, but citizens hope to influence their elected officials to vote according to the wishes of the people.

AMERICASPEAKS

AmericaSpeaks, a nonprofit organization founded in 1995, encourages citizens to gather together at town hall meetings to discuss important government issues. The organization began over growing concern that US citizens were being shut out of decision-making processes. It seeks to incorporate citizens more directly into the democratic process.

In an indirect democracy, sometimes the people elect representatives, and other times representatives are appointed by a parliament or legislative body. There has been debate on whether representatives of the people should vote according to their own convictions and conscience, or vote according to the opinion of the majority of the people they represent.

A semi-direct democracy is a combination of elected representatives voting in a legislature and citizens voting directly on some issues and referendums. The United States has been characterized as a semi-direct democracy. It has an indirect government at the federal level. On the local and state levels, there is a combination of indirect and direct forms. Semi-direct democracies include representative democracies, liberal democracies, federal republics, constitutional democracies, constitutional republics, and parliamentary democracies—closely overlapping terms that all define systems in which supreme power lies in the citizens, who then select others to act on their behalf. An immensely diverse world, however, has added new categories to democracy.

SHADES OF MEANING

There are several categories and terms for democratic governments.

- Representative democracy is an overarching term that includes any government system in which citizens elect others to govern them.
- Federal republic is basically a synonym for representative democracy, except that a republic cannot have a monarch as a head of state.
- A liberal democracy is a form of representative democracy with a strong focus on individual rights and freedoms.
- A constitutional democracy is one in which the government's structures and powers are outlined and limited by a constitution.
- A parliamentary democracy is one in which a parliament, an elected body of legislators, elects the prime minister, or head of government.

Islamic Democracies

When Arab nations began adopting democracies, a new type of democracy was created—Islamic democracy. However, two distinct types of Islamic democracies exist. One type recognizes Islam as its national religion, but religion does not interfere with the affairs of the state. Nations with this type of democracy currently include Mali, Kazakhstan, Tunisia, and Turkey. In these countries, the principles of Islam are applied only to personal and family matters. A second type of Islamic democracy combines Islamic religious law with the constitution. Sometimes Sharia, the religious laws and principles based on the Koran, have more authority than the constitution.
As of 2010, countries that combine a constitution with Sharia include Pakistan, Indonesia, Afghanistan, Egypt, Nigeria, Sudan, Mauritania, Malaysia, and Iran.

When Pakistan adopted a democratic constitution in 1956, it declared Islam its state religion, and the religion's rules have impacted government's laws and citizens' ways of life. Pakistan belongs to the United Nations (UN) but is also a member of the 57-nation Organization of the Islamic Conference. The organization works to preserve Islamic values in society and government. Nations that are part of the conference have governments that are compatible with Sharia.

Constitutional Monarchies

A constitutional monarchy is considered a democracy, although a monarch still reigns as the head of state. When a monarch is the only power in government, it is called an absolute monarchy. In a constitutional monarchy, however, a monarch's powers are limited by a constitution. Most modern monarchs in constitutional monarchies serve as rulers in title only. Most constitutional monarchies also have a parliament or legislative body and a prime minister, all elected by popular vote.

Some modern constitutional monarchies include Australia, Canada, Denmark, Japan, Kuwait, Morocco, the Netherlands, Norway, Sweden, and the United Kingdom. In most of these countries, a prime minister handles the daily leadership duties of government, while the king or the queen holds a position of honor and ceremony.

Pseudodemocracies

Sometimes a country tries to make its government appear to be a democracy. Dictatorships and Communist and fascist regimes have sometimes hidden behind a veil of what looks like a democratic structure. Citizens are granted the right to vote in a system of elected representatives. But in reality, the people participate very little or not at all in government. The government is based on the theory that the interests of the individual and the state are one and the same. It says that the state will make all the decisions for the country. It claims the state is carrying out the general will of the people. The idea is sometimes called totalitarian democracy—two words that contradict each other and struggle to stand together.

Other pseudodemocracies can develop when a democratic election results in an authoritarian leader or when an election process is corrupt. Iran's government is a theocratic republic. Citizens are allowed to vote for a president, but supreme power rests in Islamic clerical leaders. Strong theocratic rule in Iran often prevents the democratic process from functioning.

In the 2005 Iranian presidential election, the majority of Iranians voted for Mahmoud Ahmadinejad, who became their elected president. In 2009, Ahmadinejad ran against popular independent candidate Mir-Hossein Mousavi. Before all the votes were counted, Iran's official news agency announced victory for Ahmadinejad. The news agency claimed he had received 63 percent of the vote. The Iranian people, along with the European Union, Great Britain, the United States, and other Western countries, claimed voting irregularities and election fraud. Ahmadinejad was declared the winner in what many considered a fraudulent election.

Ahmadinejad defended his "completely free" reelection and called it "a great victory."[1] But Mousavi stated,

> I'm warning I will not surrender to this dangerous charade. The result of such performance

President Mahmoud Ahmadinejad of Iran was declared the winner of a contested 2009 election.

by some officials will jeopardize the pillars of the Islamic Republic and will establish tyranny.[2]

He urged his supporters to dispute the vote nonviolently; still, thousands of Iranians took to the streets, clashing with police, burning barricades, and shouting "Down with the dictator!"[3] Police responded with tear gas and violence. Many protestors were arrested, and 20 to 30 demonstrators were confirmed killed. However, Ahmadinejad won out, and in August he was sworn in for his second presidential term.

Democracy: A Legal Right

Several recent international conferences on human rights have declared democracy a legal right for all people. Their declarations are based on the Universal Declaration of Human Rights, adopted by the UN in 1948. Article 1 of the Declaration states, "All human beings are born free and equal in dignity and rights."[4]

In 1966, the UN adopted the International Covenant on Civil and Political Rights. It was signed and ratified by 162 nations. The nations agreed to respect the rights of individuals, including the right to life, freedom of religion, freedom of speech, freedom of assembly, the right to hold fair elections, and the right to due process and a fair trial. Other organizations around the globe, such as the National Endowment for Democracy, Freedom House, and the Council for a Community of Democracies, are currently working to transform dictatorships into democracies and bring freedom to oppressed countries. ⌘

"It has become ever clearer that, whatever its limitations, there is something irresistibly potent about democracy as a political rallying cry, and that any hope of halting it permanently in its tracks is utterly forlorn."[5]

—John Dunn, Democracy: A History, *2006*

Individual Rights

Today, democracies are commonly measured by the freedoms their citizens have. Oddly, the constitution of the first major democracy, the United States, did not include individual rights at first. In fact, many Americans were strongly opposed to granting specific freedoms in the Constitution. James Madison, principal author of the US Constitution, was one of them. He claimed a list of rights was unnecessary because the Constitution itself was a bill of rights. The new government, he believed, had no power to violate personal freedoms. Madison and other leaders also believed it was the responsibility

James Madison, author of the Constitution and fourth US president, was originally opposed to creating the Bill of Rights.

of the states to provide protection of individual rights.

The Anti-Federalists, who were already opposed to a strong central government, did not agree, however. They believed the Constitution was vague, weak, too short, and lacked protection against tyranny. They wanted specific, inalienable rights of the people clearly defined in the document. They were convinced that if the US Constitution did not grant specific freedoms, the federal government could easily deny those rights to Americans. They were relentless in their insistence that specific freedoms be included in the US Constitution.

Even Thomas Jefferson, a strong supporter of the Constitution, told Madison in a letter that a bill of rights was "what the people are entitled to against every government on earth . . . and what no just government should refuse."[1] Madison, now the leading member of the House of Representatives, received hundreds of proposed changes to the Constitution from the states and from Anti-Federalists. Finally, he was convinced that the Constitution should include a bill of rights. He wrote 17 proposed amendments to the Constitution that would ensure personal freedoms. He later reduced them to 12. By December 15, 1791, three-fourths of the states had ratified ten of the 12 amendments. Those ten amendments, now the first ten amendments to the Constitution, became known as the Bill of Rights, the American people's charter of freedom. They ensured important freedoms and rights that citizens of the United States would call upon for centuries to come.

Other Declarations of Rights

Other countries soon followed the United States' example of a bill of rights. While Madison was drafting the US Bill of Rights, the people of France were preparing to revolt. They were also drafting their own Declaration of the Rights of Man and of the Citizen. On July 11, 1789, Marquis de Lafayette, a French general, presented the document to the National Assembly, the citizen group that had claimed a government by the people. The document defined individual rights, declared equality for all men, and restricted the power of the monarchy. All male citizens were given the right to participate in the legislative process. It included freedom of speech and freedom of the press and made random arrests illegal.

"The people are the only legitimate fountain of power, and it is from them that the constitutional charter, under which the several branches of government hold their power, is derived."[2]

—*James Madison*, The Federalist No. 49

Thirty-three years later, in 1822, modern Greece adopted its first democratic constitution. The first section described the religious and individual rights of Greek citizens. The other sections

UNIVERSAL DECLARATION OF HUMAN RIGHTS

On December 10, 1948, the UN adopted the Universal Declaration of Human Rights. The document was inspired by the atrocities committed by Nazi Germany during World War II. It became the first international declaration of rights for all human beings. Thirty articles define what rights all human beings are entitled to have. Some of them are similar to the freedoms in the US Constitution and Bill of Rights. Article 1 states,

> All human beings are born free and equal in dignity and rights. They are endowed with reason and conscience and should act towards one another in a spirit of brotherhood.[3]

Other articles include freedom of religion, expression, and peaceful assembly; the right to life and liberty; and a fair trial.

created legislative and executive branches of government. Finland declared its independence in 1917 and enacted a constitution in 1919. The constitution laid the foundation for a representative democracy that afforded human dignity and inalienable individual rights to the Finnish people.

Individual rights became an international matter in 1948 when the UN passed the Universal Declaration of Human Rights. Two years later, in 1950, Europe collectively agreed on the Convention on Human Rights, a treaty to protect the fundamental freedoms and rights of all Europeans. That same year, India became a democracy and created a constitution that contained a charter of freedoms called Fundamental Rights. Citizens of India were

Freedom of religion allows a US citizen to practice a religion as he or she chooses—or not practice one at all.

guaranteed civil liberties that would allow them to live in peace. Ten years later, Canada passed a bill of rights, followed by Brazil, New Zealand, South Africa, and the United Kingdom.

The First Amendment Freedoms

Although every democratic constitution or bill of rights is worded differently, they all guarantee essentially the same freedoms. Most of those freedoms are based on the US Bill of Rights. The First Amendment, which ensures the freedom of religion, speech, press, and peaceful assembly, states,

> *Congress shall make no law respecting an establishment of religion, or prohibiting the free exercise thereof; or abridging the freedom*

of speech, or of the press; or the right of the people peaceably to assemble, and to petition the Government for a redress of grievances.[4]

- **Freedom of Religion.** Freedom of religion was important to Americans and many of the democratic nations that followed. Some of the first colonists, the Puritans and Separatists, left England and sailed to America to escape religious

TOWARD A COMMUNITY OF DEMOCRACIES

Representatives from 106 nations met in Warsaw, Poland, on June 27, 2000, for a conference called Toward a Community of Democracies. They declared their commitment to the UN's Universal Declaration of Human Rights and recognized the universality of democratic values. The nations agreed to a 19-point declaration of the core principles of democracy. The first point stated in part: "The will of the people shall be the basis of the authority of government," exercised through fair elections with universal suffrage.[5]

Other declarations echoed the foundations of democracy:

The right of every person to equal protection of the law . . .

The right of every person to freedom of opinion and expression . . .

The right of every person to freedom of thought, conscience and religion . . .

The right of every person to freedom of peaceful assembly and association . . .[6]

Also included were the rights to exchange ideas and information across countries, to have equal access to education, and to use electronic communication free of unlawful interference. The document ended with a commitment to promote democratic government throughout the world.

persecution and worship as they pleased. In England, the Puritans had tried for years to change the state-run Church of England. They were harassed for their attempts to change the church. The Separatists did not want to be forced to attend the Church of England at all. They wanted the right to establish their own church and worship in their own way. Making sure the US government could not establish a state religion or interfere in any individual's style of worship was important to Americans.

- **Freedom of Speech and the Press.** Freedom of speech and the press are also essential rights in a democracy. Freedom of speech and the press created the opportunity for Americans to say or write what they wanted, including criticizing the government, without fear of censorship or punishment. The nation's founders believed in free expression of ideas, whether positive or negative. Free expression helps foster an informed citizenry—a key idea when citizens are responsible for shaping the public debate around key issues of concern. Additionally, a free press can serve as a watchdog on government; some have even called the US free press the "fourth branch" of government, as it provides further checks and balances for those in power.

   During the Watergate scandal of 1972 to 1974, US citizens saw just how powerful the media could be in preventing abuses of power. On June 17, 1972, five men were caught burglarizing the offices of the Democratic National Convention at the Watergate Hotel in Washington DC. When it was discovered that the men were members of a special White House unit, the White House moved quickly to distance itself from the event, and, for a time, this strategy was successful. President Richard Nixon even went on to win a second term in office.

Then, several months into President Nixon's second term, *Washington Post* reporters Bob Woodward and Carl Bernstein began writing groundbreaking stories about what they discovered was a long pattern of illegal activities tied to the break-in. Those activities implicated the president himself. On August 9, 1974, President Nixon resigned from office in the face of certain impeachment by Congress. The *Washington Post* went on to earn a Pulitzer Prize for Public Service.

- **Freedom of Assembly.** The First Amendment also provides the freedom of peaceable assembly. This right has often been interpreted as the right to peaceful protest or the right to strike. Citizens of democracies with this right are allowed to gather publicly in a group to exchange ideas or to express or promote a common belief or interest. People are also allowed to petition the government to change something. Citizens are free to

Gathering to peaceably oppose or support a cause is a right guaranteed by the US Constitution.

join together in person or by presenting a signed document to express their views on an issue and present it to the government.

- **Due Process of Law.** Another common right in democracies is due process of law, or the fair treatment by government in legal proceedings. One part of due process of law includes a fair trial. Trials judged by a jury began in ancient

Greece. Greek juries were chosen at random and consisted of 501 to 1,501 citizens, depending on the nature of the charges. Today in Greece, a panel of three judges and four jurors decide the outcome and the penalty for committers of serious crimes. England had an early jury system, which was confirmed by the Magna Carta in 1215.

When the United States created its Bill of Rights, the judicial process, including trial by jury, was included in the Fourth through Eighth Amendments to the Constitution. The colonists had frightening memories of the British bursting into their homes and rummaging through their belongings. The British were looking for any evidence to justify arresting the colonists. The Fourth Amendment prohibits any "unreasonable searches or seizures."[7]

The Fifth Amendment states that Americans cannot be tried twice for the same crime. They also do not have to testify against themselves. The Sixth and Seventh Amendments guarantee the accused a speedy public trial with witnesses and an impartial jury. The Eighth Amendment prohibits excessive bail and any cruel or unusual punishment.

Most democracies throughout the world today give their citizens the right to a fair jury trial; however, the jury process differs widely from country to country. Great Britain and the United States are the only countries that consider a jury trial a fundamental civil right. Both countries allow the accused to choose between a trial by a judge or by a jury. Other countries allow jury trials but do not consider them an undeniable right. In fact, India, a democratic nation, abolished jury trials in 1960, on the grounds that the public and the media influenced them.

Under the Law

Individuals in a democracy are free, but they still live under a set of laws. With freedom comes the responsibility to live a lawful existence that allows others to peacefully pursue their own happiness. Laws in a democracy limit individuals' freedom in many ways—from requiring them to pay taxes or serve in the military, to mandatory immunizations and seat-belt laws. Often lawmakers must weigh individual rights against the common good. For example, in the case of seat belts, does an individual's objection to wearing a seat belt outweigh the costs incurred by society to care for those who, for lack of wearing a seat belt, end up seriously injured? Should the state be allowed to outlaw or limit an individual's use of harmful substances, such as alcohol or marijuana? Even within the purview of First Amendment rights, there are gray areas. As Supreme Court Justice Oliver Wendell Holmes Jr. famously said, screaming "fire" in a crowded theater in the absence of any real fire does not qualify as free speech. Nevertheless, in any vibrant democracy, the debate continues regard-

DEMOCRACY

ing the tension between laws and individual rights.

In democratic nations throughout the world, people are considered equal under the law. All citizens are subject to the same laws, and no individual can legally receive special privileges. The front of the United States Supreme Court building in Washington DC has these words engraved: "Equal Justice Under Law." The phrase most likely came from the 1891 Supreme Court case *Caldwell v. Texas*. The decision was summarized with these words: "No State can deprive particular persons or classes of persons of equal and impartial justice under the law without violating the provisions of the Fourteenth Amendment to the Constitution."[8]

DEFENDER OF FREEDOM OF SPEECH

The US Supreme Court has repeatedly upheld the right to free speech, either oral or written, and freedom of the press in numerous court cases. Supreme Court Justice Oliver Wendell Holmes Jr. was a mighty defender of freedom of speech during his 30 years on the high court (1902–1932). He did not, however, consider freedom of speech an absolute freedom. He ruled to restrict speech if it posed a clear and present danger, or a threat to the safety and freedom of others. Although freedom of speech and the press have sometimes been controversial, they remain important individual liberties.

The Importance of Individual Participation

Individuals may be required to live

according to the law, but participation in other areas of democracy is not required. However, an active, informed, and educated citizenry is a key component of democracy. Without an effective and involved citizenry, democracy will fail because it is a government driven by the people.

Similarly, a democracy depends on entrepreneurs and innovative thinkers to drive free enterprise and create privately owned businesses. The government does not control the economy of a democracy. As with the government, it is driven by the people. As history has shown, democracy can be threatened by a weak or failing economy. Alternately, a vibrant economy can spur a vibrant democracy. ⌘

AN ANCIENT IDEA

The words "Equal Justice Under Law" may have also come from Pericles, a leader in ancient Athens, where equal justice was important to their democracy. The following words of Pericles were spoken at his funeral in 429 BCE: "If we look to the laws, they afford equal justice to all."[9]

8

The Right to Vote

In his 1947 book, *Capitalism, Socialism and Democracy*, economist Joseph Schumpeter stated his theory of democracy:

> [The] democratic method is that institutional arrangement for arriving at political decisions in which individuals acquire the power to decide by means of a competitive struggle for the people's vote.[1]

In other words, people campaign to get people to vote for them; if they win, they gain the power to make political decisions. Schumpeter's theory was debated, but it caught on and others

---

Lawyer Inez Milholland Boissevain led a suffrage parade in Washington DC on March 3, 1913.

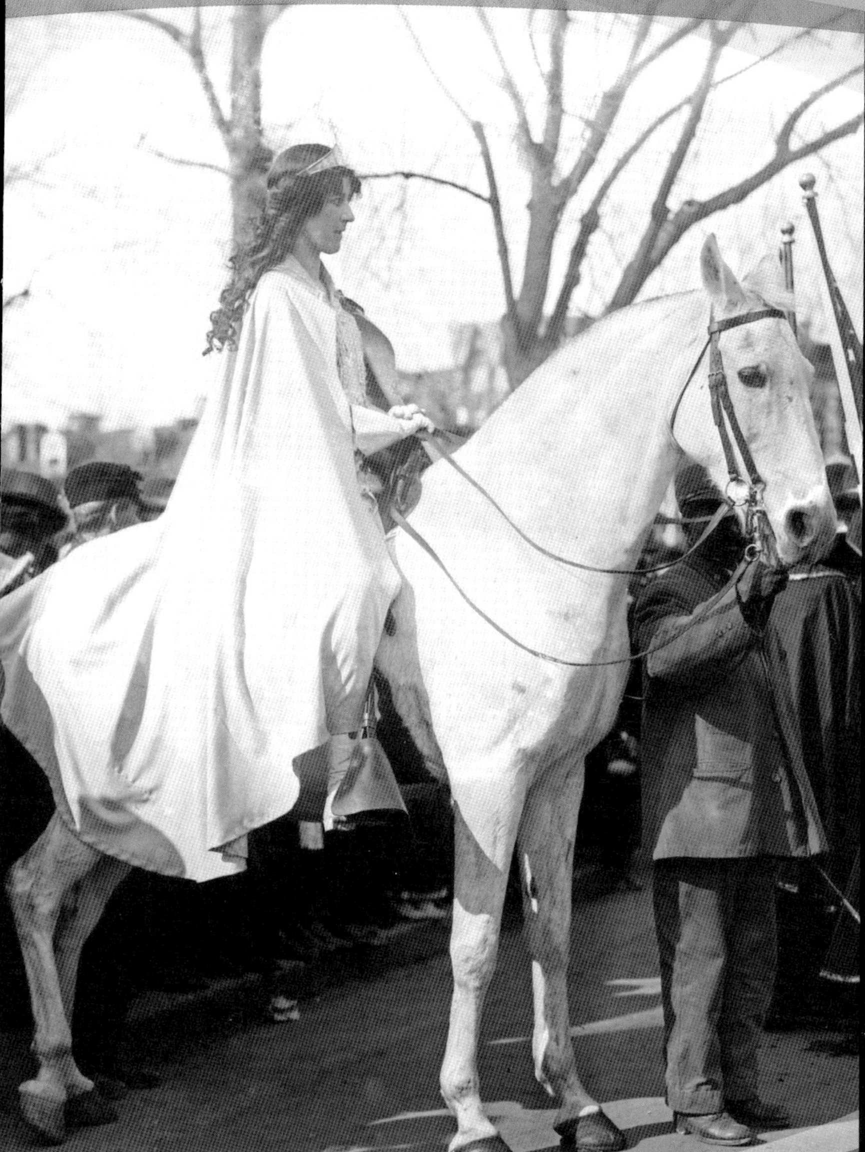

depended on it to determine if a nation was truly democratic.

Prominent political scientist Samuel P. Huntington defined a twentieth-century political system as democratic if

> its most powerful collective decision makers are selected through fair, honest, and periodic elections in which candidates freely compete for votes and in which virtually all the adult population is eligible to vote.[2]

In other words, democracies must have elections, and all citizens must be allowed to vote.

Universal Suffrage

Schumpeter's theory and Huntington's definition point out another basic tenet of democracy—the right to vote. With this classification method in place, it became easier to put a democratic label on a nation. However, many democracies and constitutional monarchies have been slow to grant universal suffrage—the right for all citizens, regardless of gender or race, to vote. In 1893, New Zealand became the first nation to grant universal suffrage. Norway allowed all men and women to vote in 1913. In 1918, at the end of World War I, Austria, Czechoslovakia, Poland, Germany, and Hungary adopted universal suffrage. The United Kingdom adopted it in 1928. France granted universal suffrage in 1944, and Japan in 1945. From 1948 to the present, the list of countries with universal suffrage has grown rapidly and includes Israel, India, Argentina,

Greece, Switzerland, South Africa, and Kuwait. Before 1971, however, Switzerland denied voting rights to women—50 percent of its population. Prior to 1994, South Africa denied blacks—70 percent of its population—voting rights.

Women's Suffrage in the United States

When the United States officially gained its independence from Britain in 1783, it immediately set up a democratic government with freedoms and rights, including the right to vote; however, only some individuals were allowed this freedom. The right for women to vote in the United States did not come until 1920. Women had begun to rally

THE ELECTORAL COLLEGE

In the United States, the president and vice president are not elected directly by popular vote. The US Constitution provides for each state to have a certain number of electors elected by state legislatures. The Electoral College, electors from all 50 states, is an example of indirect election. Although citizens of the United States cast their ballots for a president and vice president, they depend upon the electors of their state to vote for the candidates who received the majority vote of the people.

Critics claim the Electoral College is not democratic. Several constitutional amendments have been proposed to change the Electoral College or eliminate it in favor of a direct popular vote. As of 2010, all of the proposals have failed to pass in Congress.

actively for suffrage in the late 1860s, after the Civil War. Women's suffrage leaders such as Susan B. Anthony and Elizabeth Cady Stanton were opposed to the Fifteenth Amendment because it gave voting rights to African Americans and not to women. Anthony spoke for many women when she said she would "sooner cut off my right hand than ask the ballot for the black man and not for woman."[3] Other suffragists such as Lucy Stone and Julia Ward Howe had been optimistic that once African-American men were given the right to vote, women's voting rights would follow soon after.

The women's suffrage movement moved along slowly. A glimmer of hope took place in 1869, when the governor of Wyoming Territory signed into law a suffrage act that gave women the right to vote. When Wyoming was admitted to the Union in 1890, it became the first US state to allow women to vote.

Over the next 25 years, the United States

ARREST OF SUSAN B. ANTHONY

In the presidential election of 1872, suffragist Susan B. Anthony was arrested for casting a vote. She was tried, found guilty, and fined $100, which she refused to pay. In an 1873 speech, she stated,

It is a downright mockery to talk to women of their enjoyment of the blessings of liberty while they are denied the use of the only means of securing them provided by this democratic-republican government—the ballot.[4]

grew rapidly. Democracy was working, but women still could not vote. In 1913, leaders of the suffrage movement used more direct tactics. Leaders such as Carrie Chapman Catt, Alice Paul, and Lucy Burns organized a huge campaign in New York City to get a constitutional amendment passed. Membership in the movement grew to more than 100,000 people.

At the height of the campaign was a 1913 suffrage parade down Pennsylvania Avenue in the bitter cold of March. The newly elected US president, Woodrow Wilson, had arrived that day; his inauguration was scheduled for the following day. Instead of throngs welcoming Wilson, hundreds of thousands of people lined the streets to watch throngs of suffragists march from the US Capitol past the White House. Most of the women wore white clothing decorated with the US flag or depicting US freedom. Some rode on white horses, others on floats that championed their cause.

WYOMING—MANY FIRSTS FOR WOMEN

Wyoming was the first state to grant suffrage to women, and it was also the first state to allow women to serve on a jury. Wyoming had the first female justice of the peace and the first female court bailiff in the country. It was also the first state to elect a female governor, Nellie Tayloe Ross, in 1924. Because of Wyoming's support of women's rights, it has been called "The Equality State."

Not all the onlookers were in favor of women's suffrage. Some hurled insults and physically attacked the women as they marched by. Army troops were brought in to put an end to the violence that left about 200 suffragists injured. But the women were not deterred. On May 10, 30,000 women and 5,000 men staged another march. The suffragist parade up Fifth Avenue drew 1.5 million spectators. In the following six months, suffragists held more than 10,000 meetings, raised nearly $100,000, and distributed more than 7 million pamphlets. Catt encouraged suffragists to "roll up your sleeves, set your mind to making history and wage such a fight for liberty that the whole world will respect our sex."[5]

In 1915, a constitutional amendment was introduced to Congress, but it was defeated. Four years later, the House of Representatives and the Senate passed the Nineteenth Amendment to the Constitution. On August 18, 1920, the amendment was ratified by the states. The amendment reads, "The right of citizens of the United States to vote shall not be denied or abridged by the United States or by any State on account of sex."[6] Catt remarked,

> This is a glorious and wonderful day. Now that we have the vote, let us remember that we are no longer petitioners. We are not the wards of the nation but free and equal citizens. Let us do our part to keep it a true and triumphant democracy.[7]

Women's Suffrage Worldwide

Women in other democracies throughout the world also had to wait and work for the right to vote. In 1906, the women of Finland were the first to receive unrestricted voting rights as well as the right to be elected to a seat in parliament. Women in Norway were given unrestricted voting rights in 1913. In the Netherlands, Dutch women were allowed to vote in 1919. The right to vote was an impassioned struggle for the women of Great Britain. In London, suffragists staged hunger strikes, set fires, and broke windows to draw attention to their cause. British women over the age of 30 were granted the right to vote in 1918, but it was 1928 before all British women were allowed to vote.

In 1944, the women of France were given the right to vote. French women had played a major role in the revolution during the late eighteenth century, but ironically, they were banned from voting for another century and a half. When the French democratic society and constitution were established after the revolution, women were "denied political rights of 'active citizenship' . . . and democratic citizenship" for more than 50 years.[8]

The women of Greece were not allowed to vote until 1934, and then only women who were literate and the age of 30 or older could vote. All adult Greek women did not have the right to vote until 1952. Women in Canada, Latin America, India, the Philippines, Japan, Scandinavian countries, and more slowly received voting rights throughout the twentieth century.

Switzerland would be the last Western nation to grant women the right to vote. In 1959, Swiss women were allowed to vote in local elections, but it would be 1971 before they could vote on the federal level.

Voting Regardless of Race

Gaining the right to vote was also a slow process for minority races. In the United States, unrestricted suffrage for African Americans took a very long time. It was 1965 before African Americans were guaranteed unobstructed access to the voting booth.

The US Congress ratified the Thirteenth Amendment to the Constitution on December 6, 1865, abolishing the practice of slavery.

VOTING IN FRANCE

The current government of France is a republic, or a representative democracy. A president is elected every five years by direct vote of the people by universal suffrage. The president appoints a prime minister; however, parliament can disapprove and force a resignation. France's legislature, the Parlement of France, is divided into a Senate and a National Assembly. Local elected officials, including mayors and city councilors, elect Senate members. The people directly elect National Assembly members.

The French constitution calls France a democratic republic—a democracy with a combination of direct and indirect voting. It guarantees "equality of all citizens before the law, without distinction of origin, race or religion."[9] The constitution also established a motto for France: "Liberty, Equality, Fraternity."[10]

Two and a half years later, former slaves were granted citizenship through the Fourteenth Amendment. Racial tension and prejudice ran high during that time. Andrew Johnson, who became president after the assassination of Abraham Lincoln, blocked attempts to grant citizenship or civil rights to African Americans. In a letter to the governor of Missouri, Johnson wrote, "This is a country for white men, and by God, as long as I am President, it shall be a government for white men."[11]

A group of African-American leaders, led by Frederick Douglass, met with President Johnson to plead for African-American suffrage, but Johnson was not moved. In the true nature of democracy, however, the Fifteenth Amendment to the Constitution was drafted. Johnson tried to obstruct the amendment, but Congress passed it in 1869. A year later, it was ratified by the states. The amendment reads:

> *The right of citizens of the United States to vote shall not be denied or abridged by the United States or by any State on account of race, color, or previous condition of servitude. The Congress shall have the power to enforce this article by appropriate legislation.*[12]

Legally, African-American men had the right to vote. But for nearly a century to come, people who opposed African-American suffrage prevented African Americans from voting through violence, intimidation, and unreasonable voting requirements. For years, southern states required literacy tests and imposed special poll taxes on

African-American men who tried to vote. By 1900, southern states passed laws or changed their constitutions to bar African Americans, poor whites, and some Mexican Americans from voting. In many states, voter turnout for African Americans was zero.

Between 1876 and 1965, local and state governments in the South passed numerous laws that segregated African Americans from white Americans. These so-called Jim Crow laws gave African Americans what was called separate but equal status. The laws segregated public schools, public transportation, and public facilities such as restrooms and drinking fountains. African Americans were barred from restaurants, parks, and public libraries. African-American children went to schools for African Americans only. These schools received less public funding than white schools. The laws were a way to get around the Fourteenth Amendment, which guaranteed equal protection under the law to all citizens.

The federal government generally let individual states decide on issues of racial segregation. In most court cases that challenged segregation, the Supreme Court upheld the separate-but-equal concept. But in 1954, in a case called *Brown v. Board of Education of Topeka*, the Supreme Court ruled that segregated public schools were unconstitutional. The following year, an African-American woman named Rosa Parks refused to give up her seat to a white man on a public bus in Montgomery, Alabama. It was the spark that set off the civil rights movement led by minister and activist Martin Luther King Jr.

Protesters fought for the desegregation of schools and for other civil rights in the 1960s.

In 1957, Congress passed a Civil Rights Act that called for a commission to investigate discrimination at the polls. Eight years later, the National Voting Rights Act of 1965 was passed. It enforced the Fifteenth Amendment and outlawed the common practices that had prevented African Americans from voting.

Black Suffrage in South Africa

Historically, other democracies around the world have denied voting rights to people because of race. During the twentieth century in South Africa, the right to vote or hold political office was a tumultuous racial issue. In the latter part of the century, constitutional amendments stripped voting rights from black men and women, took away black representation in Parliament, and separated blacks from other races in a policy of racial segregation called apartheid.

Democracy and equal voting rights for men and women of all races did not happen in South Africa until 1994. After intense negotiations between South Africa's President F. W. de Klerk and black antiapartheid activist Nelson Mandela, apartheid ended and voting rights for blacks were restored. That year, in South Africa's first completely democratic election, Mandela was elected president. He served from 1994 to 1999.

The Voting Process

The power of the vote was unmistakable in South Africa. In the first year of restored voting rights for blacks, a black president was elected in a surprising, unprecedented free election. Voting is an important and essential part of the democratic process. It is a formal expression of the people's will as they cast their ballots for representatives, leaders, and laws. Because democracy is founded on equality, all citizens must have the same right to vote.

Each democracy has its own election process. Representative forms of government select their government officials through fair, competitive elections. A candidate usually runs for office as a member of one of several political parties. For example, in the 2009 Indonesia elections, there were candidates from 38 political parties. The candidate who receives the most votes is the winner. Elections are held every few years, with the time depending on if it is a presidential, representative, or other type of election.

Many democracies have multiparty political systems. Many of them also base their election processes on the US model. In the United States, presidential elections are held every four years; elections for senators and representatives take place every two years. In addition, each state has its own

UNIQUE 2008 ELECTION

Between 1960 and 1995, average voter turnout in the United States was only 54 percent. In the 2008 presidential election, voter turnout rose to 56.8 percent, the highest in more than 30 years.[13] Several unique aspects of the election may have caused more people to cast their ballots. It was the first election in which an African American, Barack Obama, was the nominated presidential candidate of a major political party. It was also the first time a woman, Hillary Clinton, was a presidential candidate in all primaries in all states, and a woman, Sarah Palin, ran as a Republican vice-presidential candidate.

elections for governors and state senators and representatives.

Some US states are moving toward a more direct form of democracy. In California, for example, the entire voting population often votes to accept or reject a proposition, called a referendum. The people's will, or the majority vote, results in a new law. In Vermont, towns typically hold yearly town meetings where people decide on local issues.

Voter Turnout Declining

People in democratic nations have worked passionately to ensure voting rights for every citizen.

2005 IRAQ ELECTION

In January 2005, Iraq held its first free election in more than 50 years to elect members of Parliament. Interim President Ghazi al-Yawar cast the first ballot, but violence was erupting within and outside the country. Insurgents vowed to wash the streets with voters' blood. Near a polling place in Baghdad, a suicide bomber blew himself up. Four other people were killed and nine were injured. By the end of the day, at least 36 Iraqis were killed in various suicide bombings. Turnout at the 28,000 polling booths was described as sporadic. In spite of the violence, al-Yawar stated,

> Deep in my heart, I feel that Iraqis deserve free elections. . . . This will be our first step towards joining the free world and being a democracy that Iraqis will be proud of.[14]

However, voting is sometimes taken for granted. Since the 1960s, voter turnout has decreased in most democracies. In Great Britain, voter turnout peaked at 82 percent in 1950. By 1997, voter turnout had dropped to 71 percent. The largest decline, however, took place over the next four years; in 2001, voter turnout plummeted to 59.3 percent.[15] Reasons for the decline were unclear, and analysts are still considering the reasons for a drop in voter participation over the years.

Although there are a variety of theories for why voting has declined, many people blame low turnout on lack of interest or a sense of contentment that makes voting seem unnecessary. When people believe their vote does not matter, voter turnout drops. Turnout is highest when there is a close race or an election has some important political significance. It is also believed that a fading loyalty to one particular political party can cause fewer voters to come out on election day. A reason for low voter turnout in some countries is fear. In 2005 in Iraq, violence deterred some voters from going to the polls. ⌘

9

Economic Systems

Historically, democracies have mostly had market economies, and as of 2009, all democratic governments had market economies. In market economies, enterprises are in direct competition with each other, which generally produces profit and economic growth.

It has been found that a market economy harmonizes best with a democratic form of government. In fact, democracy has endured only in countries with market economies. Democracy has never endured in countries with centrally planned economies, or ones heavily managed by the government. Centrally planned economies are closely associated with dictatorial regimes.

Sales are one way that businesses compete with each other for customers.

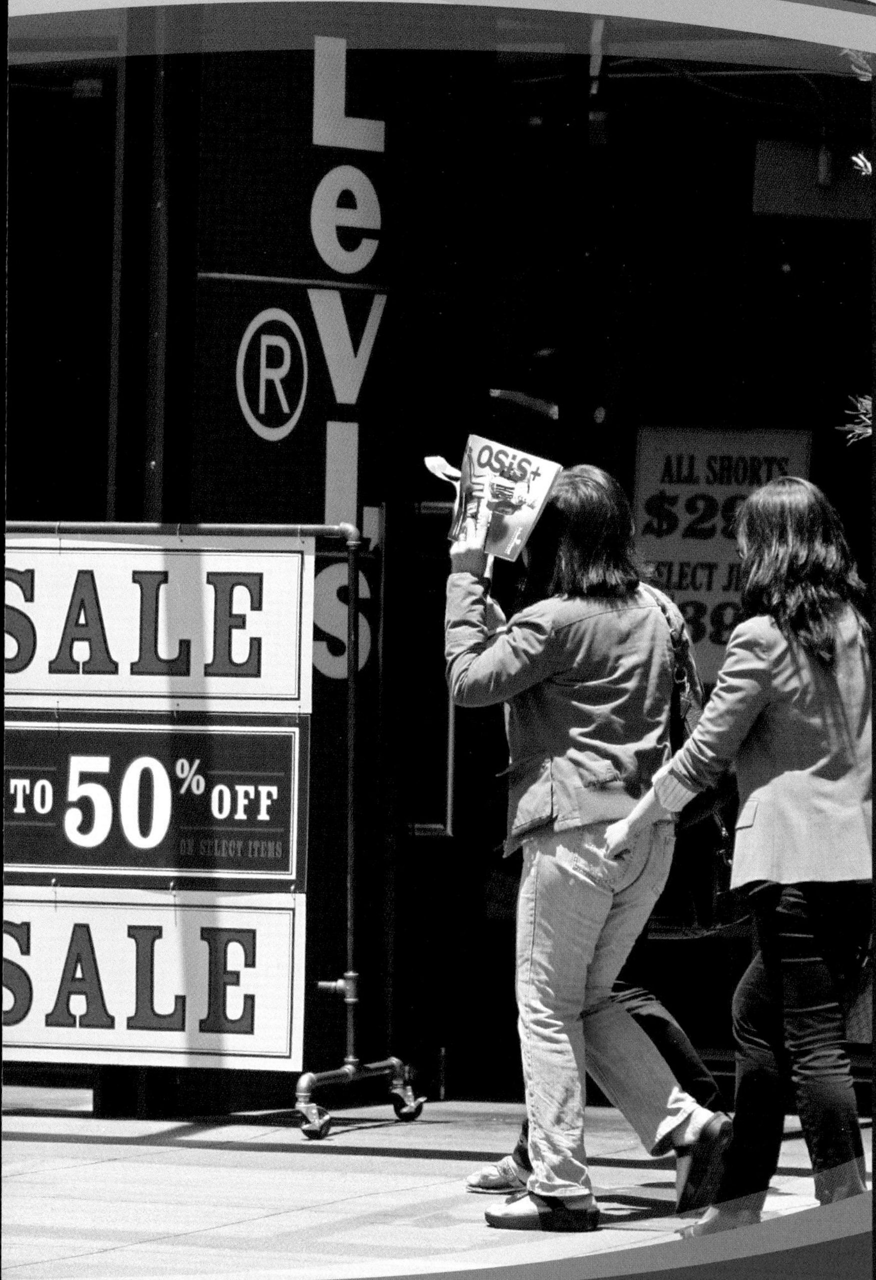
Levi's
®
SALE
TO 50% OFF
ON SELECT ITEMS
SALE
ALL SHORTS

Capitalism

Many democratic countries can be classified as having capitalist economies. Capital is wealth in the form of money or property. In a capitalist economy, industries compete with one another for their own financial gain. Businesses in a capitalist economy are typically owned and controlled by private citizens or groups, not by the government. Business owners set their own prices for goods and services based on the economic concept of supply and demand. Supply is the amount of goods businesses are willing and able to sell at a particular price. Demand, on the other hand, is the amount of goods buyers are willing and able to buy at a specific price. If demand for a certain good or service increases, meaning more people want it, then the price can increase as well. This attracts new businesses that can also

SUPPLY AND DEMAND

Starbucks Corporation is an example of how supply and demand works in a capitalist economy. In 1971, three individuals opened a Starbucks coffee shop in Seattle, Washington. Starbucks offered gourmet coffee at a high price, which was a new idea at the time. Consumers liked the coffee, and demand grew. Starbucks became extremely successful and eventually opened more than 17,000 shops in 49 countries. Other businesses started offering gourmet coffee. Competition and saturation of the market drove the supply up. Supply became greater than consumer demand. In 2008 and 2009, Starbucks closed more than 1,000 coffee shops and cut back on plans to expand.

supply the item, which increases the supply and brings the price of the item back down.

Lively competition among businesses to attract buyers to their products and prices is the backbone of capitalism. Businesspeople in a market economy expect to set their own prices, decide how much product they will produce, and run their own businesses without much government interference. However, government sometimes interferes to regulate certain industries and to protect consumers and the environment. The government also ensures robust and fair competition among businesses by outlawing monopolies.

Critics of capitalism claim that private industries breed an unfair distribution of wealth that can lead to unlimited power. They argue that excessive incomes and personal fortunes will lead to the wealthy having too much control, which could cause a capitalist economy to collapse. Critics cite examples of huge corporations that have evolved into monopolies; they take control of certain products or services and block competition. Other critics claim that capitalism has no structured plan and is thus an unreasonable way to run an economy.

When a Market Economy Crashes

History has shown that market economies can be fragile because they are based on what normal people buy, sell, and invest. Greece is a current example of a fragile market economy. One of the strongest economies in the world suddenly found itself in crisis in May 2010. Decades of overspending, inflated salaries, and rising national debt contributed to the economic collapse. Greek protestors rioted in the streets of Athens, and Europe and the United States feared a domino effect that would send their economies reeling. The United States had already experienced its own financial crisis, which had affected most of the world.

MIDDLE CLASS

Countries with privately owned businesses tend to produce large, strong middle classes. History has shown that a strong middle class tends to participate more in political affairs. Aristotle believed the middle class was extremely important to a democracy. Because the very rich tend to rule over and enslave the very poor, he concluded that a large middle class was desirable. He said that democracies are "safer and more permanent . . . because they have a middle class which is more numerous and has a greater share in the government."[1]

The Great Depression

In the 1920s, the US economy was booming. People were buying and selling commodities and trading enthusiastically in the stock market. People rushed to be part of what is called a bull market, an extended period of time when stock and gold prices consistently increase. People were eager to get rich quick.

In early October 1929, the price of wheat dropped suddenly. By October 24, numerous other industry stock prices had dropped to 1927 levels. President Herbert Hoover issued an optimistic statement to the American people: "The fundamental business of the country, that is production and distribution of commodities, is on a sound and prosperous basis."[2] A month later, however, the stock market had not recovered, and stock prices continued to drop. Hoover made another statement, both encouraging and admonishing US citizens: "Any lack of confidence in the economic future or the basic strength of business in the United States is foolish."[3]

The entire world was affected by the sudden collapse of the US stock market, which would not recover for ten years. It came to be called the Great Depression. Some called it the Hungry Years. Unemployment skyrocketed. By 1932, 12 million people—24 percent of the US population—were out of work.[4] Although the causes of the Great Depression have been debated for years, the depression demonstrated that a market economy is fragile and can crash quickly.

THE GRAPES OF WRATH

While capitalism allows for booming economic times, it also allows for recessions and depressions. Author John Steinbeck memorialized the experiences of the United States during the Great Depression through the story of the fictional Joad family in *The Grapes of Wrath*. He described Americans eating at soup kitchens, standing in bread lines, and living in shantytowns mockingly called "Hoovervilles."

*Home foreclosures increased during
the 2008 economic recession.*

There would be other times that the stock
market would drop suddenly. In the mid-1980s,
the US economy was extremely strong, but on
October 19, 1987, stock prices plunged. The crash
affected the entire world, and all major world
markets plummeted. People feared another
Great Depression, but hard work to avoid the
mistakes of the 1930s helped the market recover
in approximately two years. Some damage was
avoided by shutting down the New York Stock
Exchange for periods of time so people could not
sell their investments in the midst of panic.

Another crash occurred in 2008. By the end of that year, 15 US banks were shut down. Their failure was largely attributed to years of subprime lending. The banks had made high-risk loans that were not being repaid. Stock prices fell drastically, and the stock exchange was shut down from time to time. But the market did not rally quickly and recover. Effects of the crash were felt all over the world. Banks closed throughout Europe, and smaller countries such as Iceland were in danger of bankruptcy. A chief executive of the Bank of England called it the "largest financial crisis of its kind in human history."[5] The head of the International Monetary Fund warned that the world financial system was teetering on the "brink of systemic meltdown."[6] As of 2010, the world is still recovering from what has been called the Crash of 2008. ⌘

Democracies on the World Stage

As with all nations, democratic countries have certain obligations, roles, and responsibilities with respect to other countries. They engage in diplomacy to negotiate disputes, or, when that fails, they partake in military conflicts. They trade, importing and exporting not only natural resources and goods but services and labor as well. They monitor travel in and out of their borders and participate in international groups to resolve issues of global concern such as climate change, refugees, overpopulation, and terrorism.

NATO Secretary General Anders Fogh Rasmussen spoke to the media about a meeting of defense and foreign ministers in 2010.

DEMOCRACIES ON THE WORLD STAGE

Democratic countries tend to be more active on the world stage than countries with other forms of government. One reason for this is that, with the major exception of China, the wealthiest and most powerful countries in the world are democracies. Economically, politically, and militarily, the United States is the most powerful nation on earth. Other powerful democracies include France, the United Kingdom, Germany, Japan, and India.

Interdependency

Democracies depend on each other for trade. They depend on each other for defense as well as support in military operations. They work together in the common effort of promoting democracy worldwide. In this way, democracies tend to be highly interdependent. Many of these areas of interdependency have been formalized through trade agreements or international organizations. These include:

- **North Atlantic Treaty Organization (NATO).** Established in 1949, in the aftermath of World War II, this political and military alliance among Western democratic nations was formed to ensure their protection from enemies. Today, NATO's 28 member countries agree to mutual defense. Simply put, if one country is attacked, the others will come to its aid.

- **Organization for Economic Cooperation and Development (OECD).** Created in

1961 and based in Paris, France, the OECD provides a forum for its 33 member countries to share their views and expertise on issues of economic growth, including, for example, how to raise living standards or boost employment levels. Membership in this group is limited to democratic nations, including France, Australia, Germany, Japan, and the United States.

- **The European Union (EU).** Officially created in 1993, the EU provides the strongest example of interdependency among democratic nations. Composed of 27 democratic nations in Europe and representing 498 million citizens, this body has united the citizens of Europe politically, economically, and culturally. Member countries share a single monetary currency—the euro. Citizens

PEACE THROUGH PROFIT

The EU's roots go back to 1950, when Italy, Germany, France, Belgium, Luxembourg, and the Netherlands formed the European Coal and Steel Community. The impetus at the time was to improve struggling economies in the aftermath of World War II. However, there was another hope as well—that joining Europe's economy would be a way to bring peace to a region that had been the staging ground for two world wars in 50 years. Since then, 21 more countries have joined what has become the EU, one of the world's most integrated and far-reaching political and economic alliances.

are also free to travel, study abroad, and live in any member country. The EU passes legislation and takes joint action on issues of concern to all member countries, such as protection of the environment and terrorism.

- **Community of Democracies (CD).** Since 2000, more than 120 democratic and democratizing nations have gathered together to exchange ideas, offer advice, and affirm the principles of democracy through this international organization. Based in Warsaw, Poland, the CD's goal is to promote the rules, norms, and institutions of democracy worldwide. Member nations, including Chile, Portugal, and Romania, are diverse.

- **North American Free Trade Agreement (NAFTA).** Finalized on January 1, 2008, NAFTA has created the world's largest free trade area. Businesses in the United States, Canada, and Mexico can import and export agricultural products, natural resources, and other goods among the three countries without paying tariffs, or taxes levied by a government on imports. Traditionally, tariffs have been in place to protect domestic producers from foreign competitors; they made imported goods cost more than domestic ones. With tariffs mostly gone, NAFTA has dramatically increased trade among the three democratic nations, deeply intertwining their economies.

Globalization

In the study of international relations, the nation-state has been traditionally regarded as the center of political power. If international relations were a chess game, then each country would be a pawn. One nation could be more powerful than another, but there would be no political entity—no piece—more powerful than the nation-state. With the growth of globalization, this view of international political dynamics is changing, and political scientists are keenly monitoring the impact of globalization on democracies.

CRITICS OF NAFTA

Economists agree that, by removing government restrictions, NAFTA has greatly increased trade among the United States and its two neighbors. However, some, including the North American's largest federation of labor unions, the AFL-CIO, have posed the question—at what cost? Trade restrictions protected US jobs, they claim. With competition among businesses as the overriding value, other values, such as labor standards and environmental protection, have fallen by the wayside.

In very broad terms, globalization means that the centers of power have shifted. Now, there are new pawns in the game of international relations—organizations and multinational corporations that transcend national boundaries. These entities are not necessarily bound to any one nation's laws. Often they govern themselves. Often, nations—including democratic ones—are bound to them.

Some argue that as the power of individual governments diminishes, democracies are threatened. In democratic governments, citizens elect representatives. However, with the major exception of the EU's European Parliament, citizens generally have no say in the governance of international bodies. Leaders in democratic governments are therefore obliged to take actions, not in response to the citizens they represent, but in response to pressure by international groups or corporations.

The International Monetary Fund (IMF) provides an example of this dynamic. This highly controversial group comprises 187 countries. Based in Washington DC, it oversees the global economy, and its stated goals include promoting economic cooperation among countries as well as reducing poverty. In this role, the IMF grants loans to developing countries. However, these loans are granted only under certain conditions. In order to accept a loan, a country may have to agree to reduce trade restrictions or privatize a public industry, such as agriculture or banking, for example. In such a case, then, it is easy to see how an elected official may end up pursuing policies to meet the conditions of the IMF—an international organization based in a foreign country—instead of his or her own constituents.

At the same time, another argument can be made that globalization promotes democracy. Organizations that operate beyond national boundaries can provide another check on the balance of power within a government. The UN, an international organization with 192 member countries, often serves as a watchdog for democratic principles and practices. Formed in 1945, at the end of World War II, its stated goals include supporting international peace as well as individual human rights.

The UN has created the International Bill of Rights, which sets the standards for human rights practices worldwide. The UN has sought to uphold those standards first, by monitoring and reporting human-rights abuses, but also by pressuring or encouraging governments to safeguard human dignity. The UN offers practical help to nations as well, offering advice, training police forces and judges, performing peacekeeping operations, and overseeing elections.

Democracies and War

Since the 1960s, scholars in the field of peace research have analyzed wars statistically. They try to identify basic social or political characteristics that would make a country more likely to go to war. They track, for example, countries' systems of government, their wealth, ideologies, and internal political situations. In general, such scholars have found that democracies participate in war approximately as often as countries with other forms of government. However, as Spencer R. Weart contends in *Never at War: Why Democracies Will Not Fight Each Other,* a marked difference arises when examining wars between fully democratic nations. While democracies have come close to full-blown war, and while regimes that somewhat resemble democracies have been

DEMOCRACY THROUGH WAR?

In 2003, the United States led an invasion of Iraq, a country in the Middle East that was under the dictatorial rule of Saddam Hussein. One of the stated goals of the operation was to overthrow Hussein and bring democracy to Iraq. The operation was successful in deposing Hussein, and, seven years later, an elected government was in place. However, religious conflict and vastly diminished rights for women have kept true democracy in Iraq an elusive goal. On August 31, 2010, when US President Barack Obama officially ended Operation Iraqi Freedom, he did not claim victory.

Many US citizens have harshly criticized the war. They point to its estimated $860 billion price tag.[2] They also point to its death toll—a total of more than 655,000 Iraqis and 4,742 US servicemen and servicewomen.[3] In their view, war is not a worthwhile method of spreading democracy. Others take an even harsher view. Political science professor James Laxer, author of *Democracy: A Groundwork Guide,* claims that democracy was used as propaganda. The US invasion was dressed up in "democratic garb" as a way of affording legitimacy to an immoral war.[4]

at war, "well-established democracies have never made war on one another."[5]

Why? Explanations are still within the realm of theory, and they can be divided into two main categories. The first category is structural reasons. Some explanation may be found in the very makeup, or power systems, of democratic societies. Government checks and balances on both sides of a conflict may stop both leaders from acting impulsively or out of passion. Also, since democratic nations are generally capitalist, two democratic nations' economies are likely deeply intertwined through trade. There may be too much profit at stake to risk a war.

The other category addresses cultural norms within democratic societies. Some theorists contend that war is abhorrent to common people, and in democracies, peace-loving citizens are able to hold back potentially corrupt or bloodthirsty leaders. To such citizens, the idea of being at war with another group of citizens like themselves would be disgraceful. Still, a third explanation points to the nature of electoral systems in democracies. Those politicians who are willing and able to negotiate the nuances and withstand the compromises required to even become elected tend to be more cautious than, say, a dictator who inherits his position.

New Threat to the West

Democracies may not fight each other, but peace is still elusive for many democratic nations, particularly the United States, because of terrorism.

Terrorists do not represent a particular country or wear military uniforms. They are individuals who act alone or as part of cells, or small, elusive, violent groups. Because terrorists dress like ordinary citizens and wander from country to country, they are hard to identify and nearly impossible to find.

In general, terrorism begins with a sense of desperation and powerlessness within an individual. Countries most likely to foster terrorism are poor. Often, chaos reigns within their borders. Within this context, extremism grows; unscrupulous and ideological leaders are able to recruit followers, often by promising heavenly rewards in exchange for their martyrdom. Organized fundamentalist schools indoctrinate children from a young age. Often, these organizations are able to provide social services that the government cannot, thereby ensuring even deeper loyalty. Meanwhile, the United States—the most powerful country in the world—and its Western allies are called the sources of the world's evil. Hatred grows.

On September 11, 2001, a day now referred to as 9/11, terrorists attacked the United States. Two hijacked commercial airplanes flew into the Twin Towers of the World Trade Center in New York City. Another hijacked plane crashed into the Pentagon. A fourth plane, believed to be off track of a path to Washington DC, plummeted into an empty field near Shanksville, Pennsylvania. Approximately 3,000 people were killed. It was difficult for the United States and other countries to fight al-Qaeda, a militant

In an act of terrorism, the Twin Towers of the World Trade Center were hit by two airplanes on September 11, 2001.

Islamic group that took responsibility for the 9/11 attacks. The group has no country and remains elusive and hard to track.

Although the United States had a new enemy, its form of government took on new importance. In November 2002, US President George W. Bush said, "The global expansion of democracy is the ultimate force in rolling back terrorism and tyranny."[6] A free world had fought Germany and Japan in World War II. It had toppled the Soviet empire in the Cold War and saw most of the nations of the Soviet bloc democratized. Now the free world works to devise a strategy to combat terrorism, a movement fostered in the absence of democracy and its associated characteristics of individual rights and economic stability. ⌘

Dominant Democracy

The end of World War II ushered in a new wave of democracy. The first wave had begun in the late eighteenth century with the American and French Revolutions. Twenty-nine democracies were established from 1776 to 1918, when World War I came to an end. However, between World War I and World War II, the number of dictators in the world increased dramatically. Authoritarian governments ruled by despots rose up in Germany, Italy, Spain, and Portugal. Tyrants reigned in Brazil, Cuba, China, Japan, and the

Germany's Adolf Hitler, left, and Italy's Benito Mussolini were dictators whose regimes were defeated by democratic powers.

Baltic states. By the early 1940s, the number of democratic nations had dropped to 12.

When World War II ended in 1945, with victory for the Allies, a second wave of democracy was ushered in. Germany was divided in half, and Western Germany was occupied by the Allies, who established a democratic government. Democracies were established in Austria, Italy, Korea, and Japan; Turkey and Greece began moving toward democracies. More democratic nations followed, including Sri Lanka, the Philippines, and Israel. By 1962, there were 36 democracies in the world.

During this period, many countries around the world were also decolonized, or liberated from the long rule of large empires. Newly independent nations chose their own systems of government; many chose democracy. In 1947, India established a democratic form of government after a long struggle for independence from Great Britain. India was an extremely diverse country with a variety of religions and social classes. They created a constitution that secured justice, liberty, and equality for all people; they set up executive, legislative, and judicial branches of government similar to the United States. Some representatives were elected by popular vote of the people, others by representatives of the people. India emerged and has endured as the world's largest democracy.

The Soviet Bloc

On the other end of the political spectrum was the nondemocratic Soviet bloc. As World War II came to an end, British Prime Minister Winston Churchill, US President Franklin Roosevelt, and Soviet dictator Joseph Stalin discussed how postwar Europe should be governed. There was talk that Stalin's Soviet Union should control Eastern Europe, but Churchill compared the idea to making a pact with the devil. Stalin promised Churchill that he would avoid making Eastern Europe into Soviet countries. But later Stalin told his fellow Soviets, "Never mind. We'll do it in our own way later."[1] And they did.

After the war, the Soviets set up Communist governments in Eastern European nations. The Soviets also set up a Communist government in East Germany. On March 5, 1946, Churchill delivered a speech at Westminster College in Fulton, Missouri, and talked about Communist rule in Eastern Europe:

> We cannot be blind to the fact that the liberties enjoyed by individual citizens throughout the United States and throughout the British Empire are not valid in a considerable number of countries. . . . In these States control is enforced upon the common people by various kinds of all-embracing police governments to a degree which is overwhelming and contrary to every principle of democracy.[2]

Churchill laid out the great advantages of living in a democracy with "unfettered elections" and "freedom of speech and thought." He called these advantages "title deeds of freedom which should lie in every cottage home."[3] Churchill feared what the Soviet Communists might do and said that "an iron curtain has descended across the continent" and a shadow "falls upon the world."[4]

Nine years later, on May 14, 1955, eight countries in Eastern Europe entered into a military alliance called the Warsaw Pact. Member states included the Soviet Union, Poland, East Germany, Czechoslovakia, Hungary, Romania, Bulgaria, and Albania, and the coalition aligned forces with the Union of Soviet Socialist Republics (USSR), which was dominated by the Communist Party.

In 1961, the Soviets built a 12-foot (3.7-m) high, 100-mile (161-km) long concrete wall through Germany and through the center of Berlin. Guard towers were placed strategically along the wall. The Berlin Wall, as it was called, twisted through Germany to divide Communist East Germany from democratic West Germany. The wall served as a way to prevent Germans under the Communist regime from escaping to a free democratic country.

THE CARE OF FREEDOM

In his first inaugural address on January 20, 1953, President Dwight D. Eisenhower encouraged the US people to courageously and sacrificially defend freedom for the United States as well as the rest of the world: "History does not long entrust the care of freedom to the weak or the timid."[5]

The Berlin Wall became a symbol of communism and restrictive, authoritarian government. It represented a much larger world conflict between the Soviet bloc and the Western world that dominated most of the second half of the twentieth century—the Cold War. Although there was never a direct military engagement, both sides worked to contain the other. The Soviet bloc fought for the spread of communism, and the Western world fought for democracy.

SEVEN DAYS TO THE RIVER RHINE

In the 1980s, the eight nations of the Warsaw Pact devised a nuclear war plan called Seven Days to the River Rhine. They planned a swift destruction of most of the Western world in a seven-day atomic war. Poland was the Soviet nuclear weapons base, where as many as 250 nuclear rockets were stored. This top-secret information was not made public until 2005, when the Polish government declassified most of its documents from the Cold War period.

Third Wave of Democracy

In the mid-1970s, during the Cold War, a third wave of democracy began. April 25, 1974, marked the beginning of the largest surge of new democracies the world had ever seen. That day, a military coup overthrew an authoritarian dictatorship in Portugal, and the people established a democracy. Crowds swarmed the streets, cheering for the victorious soldiers and placing carnations in the barrels of their rifles. The coup came to be called the Carnation Revolution.

Democracy in Portugal unleashed the spread of democracy. It spread first to other European countries of Spain and Greece, and then to the Latin American countries of Brazil, Ecuador, Peru, and Bolivia. Democracy spread through Asia in 1986, first to the Philippines where the dictatorship of Ferdinand Marcos was toppled. Then it went to Korea. Over a period of 15 years, approximately 30 countries in Europe, Asia, and Latin America successfully transformed their governments into democracies.

Near the end of the 1980s, the wave of democracy engulfed the Communist countries of the Soviet bloc. It began on June 12, 1987, when US President Ronald Reagan spoke at the seven

VIOLENCE ON PATH TO DEMOCRACY

In his book *From Voting to Violence: Democratization and Nationalist Conflict,* Jack Snyder examined how, historically, the transition to democracy has prompted some of the world's most violent struggles. In particular, with the end of the Cold War in 1989, conflict between rival ethnic groups—from Burundi in Africa to Serbia in Europe—reached tragic proportions in the 1990s. Snyder explained how the rise of democracy exacerbated such disputes. For example, elections gave rise to political parties formed specifically around ethnic identities. In this way, factions that had been less pronounced under the previous government became institutionalized. Meanwhile, the free press allowed demagogues—leaders who make false claims in order to gain power—to spew dangerous rhetoric, further deepening divisions. The transition to democracy can be chaotic. Nationalist politicians offered a sense of security to citizens as they made the painful adjustment to a market economy and international interdependence.

hundred and fiftieth anniversary celebration of the city of Berlin. He stood in front of the Brandenburg Gate, the historic entrance to the city. Also behind him was the Berlin Wall. Graffiti on the wall made it clear that the people wanted freedom. Along a nearby fence hung white crosses with the names of Germans who had lost their lives trying to escape from East Berlin.

Reagan's advisers discouraged him from referring to the wall in his speech. Tensions were high between Western democratic nations and the USSR. But Reagan insisted on mentioning the wall. About halfway through his speech, he addressed Mikhail Gorbachev, General Secretary of the Communist Party of the Soviet Union, who was sitting behind him on the platform:

> There is one sign the Soviets can make that would be unmistakable, that would advance dramatically the cause of freedom and peace. General Secretary Gorbachev, if you seek peace, if you seek prosperity for the Soviet Union and Eastern Europe, if you seek liberalization: Come here to this gate! Mr. Gorbachev, open this gate! Mr. Gorbachev, tear down this wall![6]

Nearly two years later, the wall was still standing. But in September 1989, people on the East Berlin side began protesting for freedom. The protests continued throughout September and October. By the beginning of November, 500,000 East Berliners had gathered at the wall. On November 9, a West German television station announced that the government of East

Germany was immediately opening the border into West Germany. East Germans clambered to get over the wall, and some demanded that guards open the gates. The gates were opened, and the people of East Germany walked through peacefully into West Berlin. There, West Germans joined them in a huge celebration.

In the weeks to come, people from all over the world brought sledgehammers and chisels to the wall. Some were there to chip away at it and be a part of its demise. Eventually, the entire wall was removed by large equipment.

Crumbling Communism

In the late 1980s and early 1990s, Communist regimes crumbled, one after another. In Poland, the Solidarity Party triumphed over Communist Party leaders in the 1989 elections. In 1990, Solidarity candidate Lech Walesa won the presidential election and replaced the Communist regime with a democracy. The victory would become a symbol of the collapse of communism in Eastern Europe.

At the end of 1989, Communist regimes crumbled in East Germany, Czechoslovakia, and Romania. In the Western world, the people of Chile ended the long dictatorial rule of Augusto Pinochet. In Panama, the US military helped end the dictatorship of Manuel Noriega. In 1990, Nicaragua's Communist regime was defeated in an election. That year, the Haitian people also elected a democratic government. As of 2010, the only Communist countries were China, Cuba, Laos, North Korea, and Vietnam.

By the late 1990s, a majority of the world's countries had democratic forms of government. In 2000, 120 of the world's 192 nations, or 63 percent, were democracies.[7] By 2009, the number of democracies in the world had dropped slightly to 116.[8] It was a typical decline following surges of democracy. Many political scientists believe there will be more democratic nations, perhaps in a fourth wave of democracy. Historically, democratic nations have not fought wars against other democracies. If that trend continues, the spread of democracy could ultimately reduce international warfare and enhance peace throughout the world. ⌘

FREEDOM IN THE ARAB WORLD

Democracies in the Arab world have developed slowly, in part because Arab states lack organizations pushing for democracy. According to the Carnegie Endowment for International Peace, unless citizen movements develop and pressure their authoritarian governments, democracy in the Arab world "remains extremely uncertain."[9]

Free to Criticize

Defenders of democracy have proclaimed it to be the best form of government. They celebrate the equality for all people, the equal justice, and the many freedoms democracy offers. One of those freedoms is the freedom of speech, which has left the door wide open for critics. People are free to speak out either for or against their government. Opinions are welcome; disapproval is allowed.

On July 3, 2010, US Secretary of State Hillary Clinton spoke in Krakow, Poland, at the tenth anniversary of the Community of Democracies. The organization works to promote democracy and human rights. Clinton named countries, some

Greek philosopher Plato was an early critic of democracy.

of them democracies, where "the walls are clos-
ing in" on groups that press for social change and
disclose government shortcomings.[1] The countries
she listed were Zimbabwe, the Democratic
Republic of Congo, Ethiopia, Cuba, Egypt, Iran,
Venezuela, China, and Russia. She warned her
audience, made up of several hundred government officials, that "we must be wary of the steel
vise in which governments around the world
are slowly crushing civil society and the human
spirit."[2] She said, "Democracies don't fear their
own people. They recognize that citizens must be
free to come together, to advocate and agitate."[3]

Criticizing Democracy

People have been free to criticize democracies
for centuries. In ancient Athens, there were
some very outspoken critics of democracy. Greek
philosopher Plato had a particularly strong distaste for the idea of democracy. He believed that
philosopher kings who pursued truth and wisdom
should rule nations. In the *Republic*, which Plato
wrote in 380 BCE, he described democracy sarcas-
tically as "a charming form of government, full
of variety and disorder."[4] He also believed that if
people had too much freedom, chaos would take
over. History and future democracies would prove
him wrong; in fact, the opposite came to be true.

Plato's mentor and teacher, Socrates,
believed democracy's main weakness was that
inexperienced men were making decisions that
would affect everyone's lives. He agreed with
Plato that democracy was a disorganized form
of government. In the writings of ancient Greek

historian Xenophon, the author called Athenian democracy undesirable because it gave the mob too much voice in government.

Critics in the Victorian Era

During the Victorian Era, in the nineteenth century, Scottish and English authors such as Thomas Carlyle, John Ruskin, Matthew Arnold, and James Fitzjames Stephen openly criticized democracy. They shared Plato's view that democracy was a disorderly government. They also believed that only a choice few—and not the masses—are fit to govern. Stephen called the people a foolish majority; the select few he referred to as the wise minority.

British author Carlyle, who called democracy an absurd social ideal, was popular with the German people. Adolf Hitler, in particular, liked Carlyle's distaste for democracy and his belief in special, charismatic leaders. In 1945, during Hitler's final

TOO COMPLEX?

One of the criticisms of modern democracies is that their complex bureaucracies have made government out of reach for average citizens. For one, the sheer number and range of government offices and functions has become simply bewildering to the average citizen. Also, the issues at stake in modern legislation—for example, stem cell research or genetically modified foods—are so technically complex that only experts can participate meaningfully in the public debate.

days, he was reading Carlyle's biography of Frederick the Great. In it, Carlyle emphasized how a strong, shrewd leader can form a nation and change a culture.

Speaking Out for Equality

The long delay in giving equal rights to all citizens has been cause for much criticism of US democracy. It was 1963, nearly two centuries after the birth of US democracy, before all US citizens were afforded the same rights. It took several constitutional amendments for African-American men to become citizens and have the right to vote. Women spoke out and protested for more than a century before a constitutional amendment gave them the right to vote.

When the United States was still in its infancy, British author Samuel Johnson criticized the new democracy, not because it was a poor form of government, but because it allowed slavery. He wrote, "How is it that we hear the loudest yelps for liberty among the drivers of Negroes?"[5]

Even after amendments were passed, inequalities continued to prevail for African Americans. Outspoken critics, utilizing their freedom of speech, would bring about change. African-American poet Langston Hughes used his poetry to speak out against inequality for African Americans and to encourage rebellion. He criticized a democracy that had not given freedom to all. In his 1949 poem "Democracy," he wrote, "Democracy will not come / Today, this

Poet Langston Hughes spoke out for equal rights for African Americans in the United States.

year / Nor ever / Through compromise and fear."[6] He ended the poem with a call for freedom: "I live here, too. / I want freedom / Just as you."[7]

In his 1963 "I Have a Dream" speech, Martin Luther King Jr. alluded to the Declaration of Independence, the Gettysburg Address, and the Bible. He mentioned them as an appeal to the basic foundations of democracy—freedom and equality—and said that African Americans would not rest until they were granted the freedoms that a true democracy allowed.

President John F. Kennedy agreed with King that US democracy was flawed. Kennedy proposed a civil rights act that prohibited discrimination and segregation. In a radio address to the nation on June 11, 1963, Kennedy called equality a moral issue that "is as old as the scriptures and is as clear as the American Constitution."[8] He went on to say:

> The heart of the question is whether all Americans are to be afforded equal rights and equal opportunities. . . . One hundred years of delay have passed since President Lincoln freed the slaves, yet their heirs, their grandsons, are not fully free. . . . And this Nation, for all its hopes and all its boasts, will not be fully free until all its citizens are free.[9]

Less than six months later, Kennedy was assassinated. His successor, President Lyndon B. Johnson, signed the Civil Rights Act, which made racial

A PLUTOCRACY?

Critics of modern democracies, especially that of the United States, contend that they are going the way of plutocracies—governments controlled by the wealthy. Critics cite the enormous cost of running a campaign. The 2008 presidential election broke all previous records with a total of more than $1 billion spent by the two main-party candidates, Barack Obama and John McCain.[10] Critics also cite the influence of wealthy special interests, such as oil companies, that contribute to candidates' campaigns. Once elected, the candidates are beholden to their financial backers, they say, instead of their constituents.

segregation and discrimination illegal, into law on July 2, 1964.

Dissent in India

India is another democratic country that has had outspoken critics from within. In 1975, India's Prime Minister Indira Gandhi refused to resign after being found guilty in court of dishonest election practices. Some people still supported her, but most Indians spoke out passionately against her and the democracy they believed was corrupt.

Opposition forces unified people to protest in a nonviolent revolution to clean up the government. Gandhi ordered their arrests, dissolved state legislatures headed by the opposition, and shut down opposition newspapers. In June 1975, Gandhi ordered the president, India's head of state or top representative, to invoke Article 352 of the constitution and declare a state of emergency. For 21 months, the Indian people's democratic freedoms were suspended. It was estimated that 140,000 people were arrested and not given a trial during that time. Gandhi seized

WORTH DYING FOR

June 6, 1984, marked the fortieth anniversary of D-Day, when Allied soldiers stormed the shores of France to liberate Europe from the Nazis. President Ronald Reagan spoke on that spot to D-Day veterans and world leaders. He said,

You all knew that some things are worth dying for. One's country is worth dying for, and democracy is worth dying for, because it's the most deeply honorable form of government ever devised by man.[11]

great power and, in her own words, brought democracy "to a grinding halt."[12]

The first large protest against Gandhi's government was called the Campaign to Save Democracy. The people proclaimed that all they had achieved was being lost.

In an interview with the press, a protest leader stated,

> The question before us is not whether Indira Gandhi should continue to be prime minister or not. The point is whether democracy in this country is to survive or not. The democratic structure stands on three pillars, namely a strong opposition, independent judiciary and free press. [The state of] Emergency has destroyed all these essentials.[13]

"The exceptional thing about the type of government called democracy is that it demanded people see that nothing which is human is carved in stone, that everything is built on the shifting sands of time and place, and that therefore they would be wise to build and maintain ways of living together as equals, openly and flexibly. Democracy . . . implied that the most important political problem is how to prevent rule by a few, or by the rich or powerful who claim to be supermen. . . . Democracy recognised that although people were not angels or gods or goddesses, they were at least good enough to prevent some people from thinking they were. Democracy was to be a government of the humble, by the humble, for the humble."[14]

—*John Keane,* The Life and Death of Democracy

In 1977, Gandhi allowed a general election to be held and released all political prisoners. The opposition united to form the Janata Party and chose a candidate to run against the unpopular Gandhi. They campaigned for human rights and said the election would determine whether India was a democracy or a dictatorship. The Janata Party candidate, Morarji Desai, defeated Gandhi soundly in the election. The people had saved India's democracy.

Preserving Democracy

India's democracy was preserved because the people spoke out, protested, and rallied their votes to elect a nonauthoritarian leader. Even when their democratic freedoms were taken away, they still exercised democracy's basic tenets and freedoms and took back their country.

Currently, the international community is working to ensure that existing democracies survive and new democracies are formed. The global community is increasingly accepting democracy as the best possible form of government. ⌘

Quick Facts

Definition of Democracy

Democracy is a form of government in which political power resides with the people, either by direct vote or by election of representatives of the people. Freedom and equality are universally accepted characteristics of this form of government.

Well-Known Democratic Countries

Direct Democracies

- Switzerland

Representative Democracies

- France
- India
- United States (Direct democratic process for certain items, such as referendums and constitutional amendments, and citizen-initiated laws through petitions)

Constitutional Monarchies

- Australia
- Canada
- Denmark
- Japan
- Norway
- Spain
- Thailand
- United Kingdom

Organization of Democracy

Democracies are organized in several ways, but each democratic country's government usually has multiple branches of government that divide power and prevent against tyranny.

Australia

- executive: monarch (British)
- legislative: Parliament (Senate and House of Representatives)

Canada

- executive: monarch and prime minister
- legislative: Parliament (Senate and House of Commons)

United Kingdom

- executive: monarch and prime minister
- legislative: Parliament (House of Lords and House of Commons)

United States

- executive: president
- legislative: Congress (Senate and House of Representatives)
- judiciary: Supreme Court and other lower courts

Main Leadership Positions

A president is elected head of state and government in a representative democracy and serves for a limited term. A prime minister is elected or appointed head of government (when there is a separate head of state, such as a titular president or monarch) in a constitutional monarchy.

Key Developers

- Athens
- United States

Historic Leaders

In his book *Politics*, written in the fourth century BCE, Greek philosopher Aristotle wrote that liberty and equality are found chiefly in democracy. In democracy, Aristotle stated that all persons share in the government's power. Thomas Jefferson was a key author of the American Declaration of Independence, which listed humans' equality and inalienable rights. James Madison wrote and advocated for the Bill of Rights, the US Constitution's first ten amendments that ensure individual rights and freedoms.

How Power Shifts

Power moves from person to person in democracies through elections. All citizens in democracies have the right to vote in elections. In representative democracies, voters elect representatives who act for citizens and have power in government for limited terms.

Economic Systems

All democracies have market economies, economic systems in which business and production are driven by market factors, such as supply and demand, and the government has little intervention.

The Roles of Citizens

Citizens in a democracy are commonly assured individual freedoms and rights in a constitution. In most democracies, all citizens can vote or run for office in free, competitive elections. Freedoms include the right of peaceable assembly and petition.

Personal Freedoms and Rights

Rights and freedoms guaranteed in democracies differ, although most fashion their list of rights after the US Bill of Rights. Some include freedoms of speech, the press, religion, and assembly. Others are the right to petition, the right to bear arms, the right to a public trial by an impartial jury, and the right to participate in fair, competitive elections.

Strengths of Democracy

- Individual freedoms
- Individual rights
- Voice in government
- Privately owned and run economy

Weaknesses of Democracy

- Individual rights and freedoms leave room for rebellion and corruption.
- Free market economies can be fragile, based on investments and private businesses; the economy can go into a recession or depression, and the stock market can crash.
- Low voter turnout can lead to corruption or unbalanced power.

Glossary

absolute monarchy
A form of government in which supreme power is held by a king or a queen.

aristocrat
A person belonging to the aristocracy, or the ruling class or nobility.

autocratic
Relating to an absolute or unrestricted ruler.

boycott
Abstaining from using or buying a product as a means of protest or force.

commodities
Items that can be used for sale, trade, or export.

commoner
Someone who does not belong to the aristocracy, the nobility, or the upper class.

communism
A political and economic system based on a classless society and collective ownership of property.

constituents
Voters; citizens or residents served by politicians or institutions.

constitutional monarchy
A form of government led by a king or a queen whose powers are limited by a constitution; considered a type of democracy.

coup
A sudden and absolute change of government either illegally or by force.

despot
A ruler with absolute power.

dictatorship
A form of government in which absolute power resides with a dictator or a small group.

direct democracy
A form of democracy in which all citizens participate directly in government.

faction
A dissenting group within a larger group.

fiscal
Relating to finances, including spending, income, and debt.

impeach
To accuse and charge a public official with an offense committed in office.

inalienable
Unchangeable and unable to be taken away; inherently belonging to a person or a thing.

nation-state
A form of political organization that usually has only one nationality of people.

representative democracy
A form of democracy in which representatives vote on behalf of the people; also called an indirect democracy or a republic.

republic
A form of government in which citizens elect people to represent them.

serfdom
A state of a person in bondage or servitude who works in return for certain legal rights.

tyranny
A form of government in which one ruler is unrestricted by law or a constitution.

Additional Resources

Selected Bibliography

Aristotle. *Politics*. New York: Cosimo Classics, 2008. Print.

Huntington, Samuel P. *The Third Wave: Democratization in the Late Twentieth Century*. Norman, OK: Oklahoma UP, 1991. Print.

Nash, Gary B. *The Unknown American Revolution: The Unruly Birth of Democracy and the Struggle to Create America*. New York: Viking Penguin, 2005. Print.

Paine, Thomas. "Rights of Man. Part Second, Combining Principle and Practice." *The Writings of Thomas Paine, Vol. II*. Ed. Moncure Daniel Conway. New York, 1894. *The Online Library of Liberty*. Online Library of Liberty, n.d. Web.

Strassler, Robert B., ed. *The Landmark Thucydides*. New York: Free Press, 1996. Print.

Further Readings

De Tocqueville, Alexis. *Democracy in America*. Trans. Arthur Goldhammer. New York: Library of America, 2004. Print.

Dunn, John. *Democracy: A History*. New York: Atlantic Monthly, 2005. Print.

Maloy, J. S. *The Colonial American Origins of Modern Democratic Thought*. New York: Cambridge UP, 2008. Print.

Woolf, Alex. *Democracy*. New York: World Almanac Library, 2005. Print.

Web Links

To learn more about democracy, visit ABDO Publishing Company online at **www.abdopublishing.com**. Web sites about democracy are featured on our Book Links page. These links are routinely monitored and updated to provide the most current information available.

Places to Visit

Independence National Historical Park

Walnut, Sixth, Chestnut, and Second Streets, Philadelphia, PA
215-597-8787
www.nps.gov/inde
The Independence National Historical Park includes several sites associated with the American Revolution in Philadelphia, Pennsylvania, including Independence Hall, the Liberty Bell, Carpenter's Hall, and Christ Church.

Old State House Museum

206 Washington Street, Boston, MA 02109-1773
617-720-1713
www.bostonhistory.org
The Old State House Museum hosts two floors of exhibitions—including tea from the Boston Tea Party—that tell the story of the role Boston played in the American Revolution.

Pilgrim Hall Museum

75 Court Street, Plymouth, MA 02360
508-746-1620
www.pilgrimhall.org
Built in 1824, Pilgrim Hall Museum is located in the center of Plymouth, Massachusetts. It houses a collection of Pilgrim possessions. Items include William Bradford's Bible, Myles Standish's sword, and the only portrait of Edward Winslow.

Source Notes

Chapter 1. Power to the People

1. Abraham Lincoln. "Gettysburg Address." *Library of Congress.* Manuscript Division, Library of Congress, n.d. Web. 1 June 2010.

2. James Madison. "The Federalist No. 10." *Daily Advertiser.* 22 Nov. 1787. The Constitution Society, n.d. Web. 4 June 2010.

3. Aristotle. *Politics.* New York: Cosimo, 2008. Print. 156.

4. Amartya Sen. "Democracy as a Universal Value." *Journal of Democracy* 10.3 (1999): 3–17. National Endowment for Democracy and the Johns Hopkins University Press, n.d. Web. 1 June 2010.

5. Freedom House. "Freedom in the World 2010: Global Erosion of Freedom." *Freedom House.* Freedom House, 12 Jan. 2010. Web. 21 Aug. 2010.

6. Ibid.

7. Arch Puddington. "Freedom in the World 2010: Erosion of Freedom Intensifies." *Freedom House.* Freedom House, 2010. Web. 26 Oct. 2010.

8. Freedom House. "Freedom in the World 2010: Global Erosion of Freedom." *Freedom House.* Freedom House, 12 Jan. 2010. Web. 21 Aug. 2010.

9. Ibid.

10. Jason Groves. "Nightmare Vision for Europe as EU Chief Warns 'Democracy Could Disappear' in Greece, Spain and Portugal." *Mail Online.* Associated Newspapers, Ltd., 15 June 2010. Web. 21 Aug. 2010.

11. "Nation: Lasting Lessons." *Time Online.* Time, Inc., 13 Oct. 1961. Web. 3 July 2010.

12. "Declaration of Sentiments." *NPS.gov.* National Park Service, 27 Oct. 2006. Web. 2 June 2010.

13. Martin Luther King Jr. *I have a Dream: Writings & Speeches that Changed the World.* Ed. James M. Washington. New York: HarperOne, 1992. Print. 102.

14. Ibid.

Chapter 2. Democracy's Foundation

1. Thucydides. *History of the Peloponnesian War.* Trans. Richard Crawley. New York: E. P. Dutton, 1910. *Google Book Search.* Web. 4 Oct. 2010.

2. Aristotle. "Constitution of Athens." London, 1891. *Online Library of Liberty.* Online Library of Liberty, n.d. Web. 18 June 2010.

3. Xenophon. "On Men and Women." *Internet Ancient History Sourcebook.* Internet History Sourcebooks Project, Aug. 1998. Web. 18 June 2010.

4. Aristotle. "Constitution of Athens." London, 1891. *Online Library of Liberty.* Online Library of Liberty, n.d. Web. 18 June 2010.

5. "Pnyx: The Site." *Serving History.* Serving History, n.d. Web. 18 June 2010.

6. Thucydides. *History of the Peloponnesian War.* Trans. Richard Crawley. New York: E. P. Dutton, 1910. *Google Book Search.* Web. 4 Oct. 2010.

Chapter 3. Traces of Democracy

1. Cornelius Tacitus. "The Annals." *Perseus Digital Library*. Perseus Digital Library Project, n.d. Web. 22 June 2010.
2. Ibid.
3. "The Magna Carta." *The National Archives Online*. National Archives & Records Administration, n.d. Web. 21 June 2010.
4. Ibid.
5. Ibid.
6. "The First Charter of Virginia; April 10, 1606." *The Avalon Project: Documents in Law, History and Diplomacy*. Yale Law School, Lillian Goldman Law Library, n.d. Web. 21 June 2010.
7. Ibid.
8. "The Mayflower Compact." *Pilgrim Hall Museum*. Pilgrim Hall Museum, n.d. Web. 22 June 2010.

Chapter 4. Revolutions for Democracy

1. Gary B. Nash. *The Unknown American Revolution: The Unruly Birth of Democracy and the Struggle to Create America*. New York: Viking Penguin, 2005. Print. 90–91.
2. "Declaration of Independence." *The Charters of Freedom*. National Archives & Records Administration, n.d. Web. 22 June 2010.
3. Ibid.
4. Ibid.
5. Ibid.
6. Thomas Paine. "Rights of Man. Part Second, Combining Principle and Practice." *The Writings of Thomas Paine, Vol. II*. Ed. Moncure Daniel Conway. New York, 1894. *Online Library of Liberty*. Online Library of Liberty, n.d. Web. 23 June 2010.
7. "Declaration of the Rights of Man – 1789." *The Avalon Project: Documents in Law, History and Diplomacy*. Yale Law School, Lillian Goldman Law Library, n.d. Web. 21 June 2010.
8. Ibid.

Chapter 5. How Democracy Works

1. John Dunn. *Democracy: A History*. New York: Atlantic Monthly, 2005. Print. 73–74.
2. "The Constitution: The 19th Amendment." *The National Archives Online*. National Archives & Records Administration, n.d. Web. 24 June 2010.
3. Robert B. Strassler, ed. *The Landmark Thucydides*. New York: Free Press, 1996. Print. 113.
4. Alexis de Tocqueville. *Democracy in America, Volume I*. Trans. Arthur Goldhammer. New York: Library of America, 2004. Print. 6.

Chapter 6. Types of Democracy

1. "Ahmadinejad Defiant on 'Free' Iran Poll." *BBC News Online.* BBC, 14 June 2009. Web. 5 July 2010.

2. Parisa Hafezi and Frederik Dahl. "Ahmadinejad's Victory Greeted by Tehran Protests." *Reuters.* Thomson Reuters, 13 June 2009. Web. 1 Nov. 2010.

3. "Ahmadinejad Defiant on 'Free' Iran Poll." *BBC News Online.* BBC, 14 June 2009. Web. 5 July 2010.

4. "The Universal Declaration of Human Rights." *United Nations.* The United Nations, 10 Dec. 1948. Web. 5 July 2010.

5. John Dunn. *Democracy: A History.* New York: Atlantic Monthly Press, 2005. Print. 17.

Chapter 7. Individual Rights

1. Roger A. Bruns. *A More Perfect Union: The Creation of the United States Constitution. The Charters of Freedom.* National Archives Online, n.d. Web. 4 Oct. 2010.

2. James Madison. "The Federalist No. 49." *Independent Journal.* 2 Feb. 1788. *The Constitution Society.* The Constitution Society, n.d. Web. 27 June 2010.

3. "The Universal Declaration of Human Rights." *United Nations.* The United Nations, 10 Dec. 1948. Web. 5 July 2010.

4. "Bill of Rights." *The Charters of Freedom.* National Archives Online, n.d. Web. 4 Oct. 2010.

5. "Toward a Community of Democracies Ministerial Conference: Final Warsaw Declaration: Toward a Community of Democracies." *Council for a Community of Democracies.* Council for a Community of Democracies, 27 June 2000. Web. 5 July 2010.

6. "Final Warsaw Declaration: Toward a Community of Democracies." *Council for a Community of Democracies.* Council for a Community of Democracies, 27 June 2000. Web. 5 July 2010.

7. "Bill of Rights." *The Charters of Freedom.* National Archives Online, n.d. Web. 4 Oct. 2010.

8. Caldwell v. Texas 137 US 692. Supreme Court of the US. 1891. *Justia.com.* US Supreme Court Center, n.d. Web. 30 June 2010.

9. Thucydides. *History of the Peloponnesian War.* Trans. Richard Crawley. New York: E. P. Dutton, 1910. *Google Book Search.* Web. 4 Oct. 2010.

Chapter 8. The Right to Vote

1. Joseph A. Schumpeter. *Capitalism, Socialism, and Democracy.* New York: Harper, 1947. Print. 269.

2. Samuel P. Huntington. *The Third Wave: Democratization in the Late Twentieth Century.* Norman, OK: Oklahoma UP, 1991. Print. 7.

3. William S. McFeely. *Frederick Douglass.* New York: Simon & Schuster, 1991. Print. 266.

4. Lewis Copeland, Lawrence W. Lamm, and Stephen J. McKenna, eds. *The World's Great Speeches.* Mineola, NY: Dover, 1999. Print. 321.

5. Jacqueline Van Voris. *Carrie Chapman Catt: A Public Life.* New York: Feminist Press, 1987. Print. 129.

6. "Constitution of the United States: Amendments 11-27." *The Charters of Freedom.* National Archives Online, n.d. Web. 4 Oct. 2010.

7. Jacqueline Van Voris. *Carrie Chapman Catt: A Public Life*. New York: Feminist Press, 1987. Print. 160.

8. Sara E. Melzer and Leslie W. Rabine, eds. *Rebel Daughters: Women and the French Revolution*. New York: Oxford UP, 1992. Print. 79.

9. "Constitution of October 4, 1958." *Assemblée Nationale Online*. Assemblée Nationale, n.d. Web. 30 June 2010.

10. Ibid.

11. "People & Events: The Impeachment of Andrew Johnson." *PBS Online*. PBS, n.d. Web. 28 June 2010.

12. "Constitution of the United States: Amendments 11-27." *The Charters of Freedom*. National Archives Online, n.d. Web. 4 Oct. 2010.

13. "National Voter Turnout in Federal Elections: 1960–2008." *Infoplease*. Pearson Education, n.d. Web. 26 Oct. 2010.

14. "Milestone Elections Begin in Iraq." *CNN World*. Cable News Network, 30 Jan. 2005. Web. 26 Oct. 2010.

15. "Low Voter Turnout—A Threat to Democracy in the UK?" *Tutor2u*. Tutor2u, n.d. Web. 22 Aug. 2010.

Chapter 9. Economic Systems

1. Aristotle. "The Polis as the Highest Good." *Internet Ancient History Sourcebook*. Internet History Sourcebooks Project, Aug. 1998. Web. 1 July 2010.

2. John Kenneth Galbraith. *The Great Crash, 1929*. New York: Houghton Mifflin, 1997. Print. 106.

3. "*Oh Yeah?*: Herbert Hoover Predicts Prosperity." *History Matters*. N.p., n.d. Web. 1 July 2010.

4. Robert VanGiezen and Albert E. Schwenk. "Compensation from before World War I through the Great Depression." *United States Department of Labor*. U.S. Bureau of Labor Statistics, 30 Jan. 2003. Web. 26 Oct. 2010.

5. Sam Fleming. "'Worst Financial Crisis in Human History': Bank Boss's Warning as Pound Suffers Biggest Fall for 37 Years." *Mail Online*. Associated Newspapers, Ltd., 25 Oct. 2008. Web. 3 July 2010.

6. Canwest News Service. "Finance Ministers Face Down Crisis as IMF Head Warns of 'Meltdown.'" *Canada.com*. Canada.com, 12 Oct 2008. Web. 3 July 2010.

Chapter 10. Democracies on the World Stage

1. "2009 Independent Auditors' Report." *National Endowment for Democracy Online*. National Endowment for Democracy, 2010. Web. 21 Aug. 2010.

2. James Glanz. "The Economic Cost of War." *The New York Times*. The New York Times Company, 28 Feb. 2009. Web. 4 Oct. 2010.

3. David Brown. "Study Claims Iraq's 'Excess' Death Toll Has Reached 655,000." *The Washington Post*. The Washington Post Company, 11 Oct. 2006. Web. 4 Oct. 2010.

4. James Laxer. *Democracy: A Groundwork Guide*. Toronto: Groundwood Books, 2009. Print. 81.

5. Spencer R. Weart. *Never at War: Why Democracies Will Not Fight One Another*. New Haven, CT: Yale University Press, 1998. Print. 13.

6. John Dunn. *Democracy: A History*. New York: Atlantic Monthly Press, 2005. Print. 158–159.

Chapter 11. Dominant Democracy

1. Simon Berthon and Joanna Potts. *Warlords: An Extraordinary Re-Creation of World War II Through the Eyes and Minds of Hitler, Churchill, Roosevelt, and Stalin.* Da Capo Press, 2007. Print. 289.

2. Winston Churchill. "The Sinews of Peace." *Sources of World History.* Ed. Mark A. Kishlansky. New York: HarperCollins, 1995. Print. 298–302.

3. Ibid.

4. Ibid.

5. Dwight D. Eisenhower. "First Inaugural Address of Dwight D. Eisenhower." 20 Jan. 1953. *The Avalon Project: Documents in Law, History and Diplomacy.* Yale Law School, Lillian Goldman Law Library, n.d. Web. 3 July 2010.

6. Ronald Reagan. "Tear Down this Wall." *The History Place: Great Speeches Collection.* The History Place, n.d. Web. 3 July 2010.

7. Freedom House. "*Freedom in the World*–Electoral Democracies." *Freedom House.* Freedom House, n.d. Web. 26. Oct. 2010.

8. Ibid.

9. Marina Ottaway. "Democracy and Constituencies in the Arab World." July 2004. *Carnegie Endowment for International Peace Online.* Carnegie Endowment for International Peace, n.d. Web. 5 July 2010.

Chapter 12. Free to Criticize

1. Robert Burns. "Clinton: 'Steel Vise' Crushing Global Activists." *The Washington Times.* The Washington Times, LLC, 3 July 2010. Web 4 July 2010.

2. Ibid.

3. Ibid.

4. Plato. *Republic.* Tran. Benjamin Jowett. Forgotten Books, 2008. *Google Book Search.* Web. 8 Oct. 2010.

5. "African Americans in the Revolutionary Period." *National Park Service.* National Park Service, n.d. Web. 4 July 2010.

6. Langston Hughes. "Democracy." *American Poems.* Gunnar Bengtsson, n.d. 4 July 2010.

7. Ibid.

8. John F. Kennedy. "Radio and Television Report to the American People on Civil Rights." 11 June 1963. *John F. Kennedy Presidential Library & Museum.* John F. Kennedy Presidential Library & Museum, n.d. Web. 4 July 2010.

9. Ibid.

10. Jeanne Cummings. "2008 Campaign Costliest in U.S. History." *Politico.* Politico, 5 Nov. 2008. Web. 4 Oct. 2010.

11. Ronald Reagan. "On the 40th Anniversary of D-Day." 6 June 1984. *The History Place: Great Speeches Collection.* The History Place, n.d. Web. 5 July 2010.

12. "Indira Gandhi Biography." *Biography Base.* Biography Base, n.d. Web. 5 July 2010.

13. Gurmit Singh. *A History of Sikh Struggles.* New Delhi: Atlantic, 1991. Print. 39.

14. John Keane. *The Life and Death of Democracy.* New York: Norton, 2009. Print. xii.

Index

Acropolis, 18, 21
African-American rights, 15,
    92, 97, 99, 139–140
age of democracy, 14
American Civil War, 8, 92
American colonies, 36–39,
    40–41, 42–48
    colonial union, 41
    Connecticut, 40–41
    Jamestown, 37–38
    Pennsylvania, 38–39, 41, 44
    Plymouth, 38
    Rhode Island, 40
American Revolution, 45–48
ancient Greeks, 8, 11, 16–27,
    30–31, 35
    Alexander the Great, 30–31
    Athenian democracy, 16–27
    Athenian military, 23–25
    Battle of Marathon, 23
    Delian League, 25–26
    Peloponnesian League,
        26–27
    Peloponnesian War, 26–27,
        35
    Thirty Tyrants, 26–27
    women's rights, 19
Annals, The, 30
Anthony, Susan B., 92
Anti-Federalists, 76–77
arengos, 32
Aristotle, 11, 35
Athens, Greece, 13,16–28, 31,
    35, 48, 56, 58, 66, 108, 136

Barroso, José Manuel, 14
Berlin Wall, 128–129, 131–132
Bill of Rights (England), 40
Bill of Rights (United States),
    40, 76–77, 79, 84

Boston Massacre, 42
Boston Tea Party, 42–44
British Empire, 45, 126, 127
*Brown v. Board of Education
    of Topeka*, 98

*Capitalism, Socialism and
    Democracy*, 88
Charles II (king), 38, 39, 40
Churchill, Winston, 34,
    127–128
Civil Rights Act, 99, 140
Cleisthenes, 18
Clinton, Hillary, 134–136
Cold War, 123, 129–133
Committee of Five, 45
communism, 13, 70, 119,
    127–133
Community of Democracies,
    73, 80, 134
Constitution, US, 10, 47–48,
    56–58, 60–63, 74–77, 78–87,
    94, 97–99, 138–139
Constitution of Athens, 35
Continental army, 45
Continental Congress, 44–45
    First, 44
    Second, 45
Council for a Community of
    Democracies, 73
Council of 500, 20
criticism, 134–142
    complexity, 137
    Greek philosophers,
        136–137
    Indian, 140–143
    inequalities, 138–139
    plutocracy, 139
    Victorian Era, 137–138
Currency Act, 44

Declaration of Independence, 11, 15, 45–47
Declaration of Rights and Grievances, 44
Declaration of Sentiments, 15
Declaration of the Rights of Man and of the Citizen, 49–50, 77
democracy
  constitutions, 48, 50, 53, 54, 56–58, 60–63, 66–70, 74–87, 90–91, 93–98, 100, 126, 138–139, 141
  equality, 11, 14, 31–32, 40, 52, 56–59, 77, 95, 100, 126, 134, 138–140
  fair elections, 10–11, 19, 37, 40–41, 48, 50, 53, 54–56, 58–59, 67–68, 70–71, 73, 80, 90–93, 95, 96, 100–103, 119–121, 126–127, 130, 132–133, 139, 143
  first wave, 125–126
  global interdependencies, 114–116
  individual participation, 19, 32, 36, 50, 58, 66, 70, 77, 87, 102–103, 108
  individual rights, 68, 74–87, 123
  laws, 21, 38, 42, 44, 56–57, 61–63, 66, 69, 85–87, 98, 100, 117
  second wave, 41, 126
  separation of power, 57, 60–63
  third wave, 129–132
  war, 8, 13, 22, 26, 28, 31, 35, 39, 47, 51, 78, 90, 92, 114, 115, 119–121, 123, 124–130, 133

democracy, types of, 64–73
  constitutional monarchies, 54, 56, 57, 69–70
  direct, 66–68
  federal republic, 67, 68
  indirect, 66–68
  Islamic, 68–69
  liberal, 67, 68
  parliamentary form, 54, 67, 68
  pseudo, 70–72
  representative form, 58, 66–67, 68, 78, 95
  semi-direct, 66–68
Democracy in America, 59
dēmokratía, 8
Diodotus, 22

Ecclesia, 20–22
economic systems, 49, 104–111, 115
  capitalism, 106–107
  fragile market economies, 107–111
Eisenhower, Dwight D., 128
Electoral College, 91
European Union, 14, 71, 115–116

Federalist, The, 10
Frame of Government of Pennsylvania, 39
Franklin, Benjamin, 41, 45
Freedom House, 12, 15, 73
French National Assembly, 49
French Revolution, 49, 50–53, 124
  Directory, 51
  guillotine, 51, 52
  Reign of Terror, 51–52
From Voting to Violence: Democratization and Nationalist Conflict, 130

Gettysburg Address, 8, 139
globalization, 117–119
Great Depression, 108–109

Haitian Revolution, 51
Henry, Patrick, 44
Henry III (king), 34
History of the Peloponnesian War, 35
Hobbes, Thomas, 39
Holmes, Oliver Wendell, Jr., 85, 86
hoplites, 23
  See also ancient Greeks: Athenian military
House of Representatives, US, 60, 76, 94

"I Have a Dream" speech, 15, 139
ideology, 10–11
impeachment, 62, 82
International Bill of Rights, 119
International Monetary Fund, 111, 118
Iroquois Confederacy, 48

James I (king), 36, 38
James II (king), 41
Jefferson, Thomas, 11, 45, 76
John, King, 32–33

Keane, John, 142
Kennedy, John F., 14, 139, 140
King, Martin Luther, Jr., 15, 99, 139

legislation, US, 58, 60–63
Lincoln, Abraham, 8, 97, 140
Lincoln Memorial, 15
Louis IX (king), 34
Louis XVI (king), 49, 50–51

Macedonians, 27–28
Madison, James, 10, 74–77
Magna Carta, 32–35, 84
Mayflower Compact, 38–39

National Endowment for Democracy, 15, 73
National Voting Rights Act, 99
Nobel Prize in Economics, 11
North American Free Trade Agreement, 116, 117
North Atlantic Treaty Organization, 114

Obama, Barack, 101, 120, 139
Operation Iraqi Freedom, 120
Organization for Economic Cooperation and Development, 114–115
Organization of the Islamic Conference, 69

Peisistratos, 18, 25
Pericles, 20, 58
Persia, 22–25, 31
Phillip II (king), 27
Pnyx, 21

Renaissance, 13, 35–36
Republic, 35, 136
right to vote, 58–59, 88–103
  racial minorities, 96–99
  South Africa, 100
  universal, 90–91
  women, 91–96
Rights of Man, 48
Roman dictators, 30–31
Roman Empire, 30–31
Roosevelt, Eleanor, 12

Schumpeter, Joseph, 88, 90
Sen, Amartya, 11

Soviet bloc, 13, 123, 127–129,
    130
Stamp Act, 44
Stanton, Elizabeth Cady, 15,
    92
Sugar Act, 44
Supreme Court, US, 61,
    86–87, 98

terrorism, 112, 116, 122–133
Thucydides, 18, 35
Tocqueville, Alexis de, 59
Toward a Community of
    Democracies, 80
Townshend Act, 44
Treaty of Paris, 46

Union of Soviet Socialist
    Republics, 128, 131
United Nations, 69, 73, 78
    International Covenant on
    Civil and Political Rights,
    73
    Universal Declaration of
    Human Rights, 73, 78
United States of America, 13,
    45, 47

Vietnam War, 13

Warsaw Pact, 128
Washington, George, 45
Washington DC, 15, 82, 86,
    118, 122
Watergate scandal, 62, 81–82
Willkie, Wendell, 12
Windsor, Jennifer, 12
women's rights, 15, 90–96
World War II, 13, 78, 114, 115,
    119, 123–127

Xenophon, 137